RACIAL PROFILING
EVERYDAY INEQUALITY

ALISON MARIE BEHNKE

TWENTY-FIRST CENTURY BOOKS / MINNEAPOLIS

Content Consultant:
Dr. Tanya Gladney, PhD
Associate Professor, Department of Sociology and Criminal Justice, and law enforcement
coordinator, University of St. Thomas, Saint Paul, Minnesota

Twenty-First Century Books
A division of Lerner Publishing Group, Inc.
241 First Avenue North
Minneapolis, MN 55401 USA

For reading levels and more information, look up this title at www.lernerbooks.com.

Main body text set in Bodoni MT Std 11/16.
Typeface provided by Adobe Systems.

Library of Congress Cataloging-in-Publication Data

Names: Behnke, Alison, author.
Title: Racial profiling / Alison Marie Behnke.
Description: Minneapolis : Twenty-First Century Books, 2017. | Audience: Grade 9 to 12. |
    Includes bibliographical references and index.
Identifiers: LCCN 2016009454 (print) | LCCN 2016010999 (ebook) | ISBN 9781512402681
    (lb : alk. paper) | ISBN 9781512428513 (eb pdf)
Subjects: LCSH: Racial profiling in law enforcement—United States—Juvenile literature.
Classification: LCC HV7936.R3 B46 2017 (print) | LCC HV7936.R3 (ebook) | DDC
    363.2/308900973—dc23

LC record available at http://lccn.loc.gov/2016009454

Manufactured in the United States of America
2-44480-21038-6/23/2017

CONTENTS

Protesters in Los Angeles, California, stage a "die-in" demonstration to raise awareness about the fatal consequences of police brutality and racial profiling.

CHAPTER 1
PREJUDICE AND PRIVILEGE

On the afternoon of November 22, 2014, a concerned Cleveland resident called 911 and reported seeing "a guy with a pistol" at a local park. He added that the gun was "probably fake" and that the person holding it was "probably a juvenile" but that the situation was making the caller uneasy. "Is he black or white?" asked the 911 dispatcher. The caller responded, "He's black." The person in question was twelve-year-old Tamir Rice, who was carrying a BB gun.

Another dispatcher relayed the caller's information to two police officers, without mentioning the caller's impressions of Rice's youth or his suspicion that Rice's gun was fake. She designated the situation as a Code 1, the highest priority emergency level.

Security camera footage from the park shows that the officers' squad car drove across the grass and pulled up to a gazebo, no more than 7 feet (2 meters) from where Rice was playing. Within two seconds, Officer Timothy Loehmann got out of the car and shot Rice once in the stomach. When Rice's fourteen-year-old sister ran to help him, officers tackled and handcuffed her. Samaria Rice, Tamir's mother, also rushed to the park. She later recalled that the officers refused to let her through to her son. "The police told me to calm down or they would put me in the back of the police car." Tamir died the next day in the hospital.

Authorities initiated multiple investigations into Tamir Rice's shooting death. A report released in June 2015 by the Cuyahoga County Sheriff's Department stated that, while the officers said they had shouted warnings to Rice before shooting him, no conclusive proof of any type of warning could be found. Nevertheless, in October 2015, two other reports conducted by outside reviewers concluded

Demonstrator Tomiko Shine *(center)* holds a picture of twelve-year-old Tamir Rice *(pictured)*, who was fatally shot by police in Washington, DC, in November 2014. His death sparked widespread calls for police accountability in cases of racial profiling and police brutality.

that Loehmann had acted reasonably in deciding to fire his weapon. And in December 2015, a grand jury ruled that Loehmann's actions were justified and that he would therefore not face criminal charges. Janai Nelson of the National Association for the Advancement of Colored People (NAACP) Legal Defense Fund blamed several related factors for the legal outcome, saying, "Rice's death and the lack of accountability for it are a result of racial profiling, incompetent 911 services, over-zealous and reckless policing practices, and a systemic bias in favor of police."

Everyday Indignities

Racial profiling was not the sole cause of Tamir Rice's death at the hands of police officers. Yet it plays a crucial role not only in Rice's tragic fate but in numerous other American lives. In the United States, racial profiling is both an everyday reality for many Americans and a hot-button issue in the national conversation about race, policing, and justice.

So what is racial profiling? The American Civil Liberties Union (ACLU), an organization that advocates for individual rights and freedoms, defines it as "the discriminatory practice by law enforcement officials of targeting individuals for suspicion of crime based on the individual's race, ethnicity, religion or national origin." Amnesty International USA, an organization that campaigns for human rights, uses a similar definition, although it clarifies that profiling can be appropriate if "there is trustworthy information, relevant to the locality and timeframe, that links persons belonging to [certain groups] to an identified criminal incident or scheme." In the United States, racial profiling typically targets African Americans, as well as people of Latino (or Hispanic), Middle

Eastern, American Indian, and Asian descent. Muslims—
followers of the religion of Islam—also frequently encounter
profiling, as do other people who are perceived to be Muslim
based on their appearance and perceived racial backgrounds.

At its most basic level, racial profiling assumes a
connection between a person's racial or ethnic background and
the likelihood that the person is prone to criminal behavior—
or otherwise deserving of distrust. Profilers—who may include
police officers, security officials, prison guards, bankers,
lawyers, and average citizens—react to the person based on
this assumption. Depending on the situation, the expression
of racial profiling can vary widely, from a suspicious look or
an aggressive comment to denial of a loan, rejection of a job
application, arrest, incarceration, harassment, physical injury,
and death.

Americans disagree on how often profiling occurs in the
United States. At some levels of law enforcement, official policy
explicitly permits racial profiling. For instance, federal agents
may legally consider race and ethnicity when stopping travelers
at airports, border crossings, and immigration checkpoints.
Federal guidelines also allow the Federal Bureau of
Investigation (FBI) to use the ethnic makeup of neighborhoods
as a basis for targeting investigations and recruiting
informants. Twenty out of fifty states have no laws banning
racial profiling by police. Even in settings where the practice
is prohibited, racial profiling can occur unofficially, and it is
difficult for victims to prove that they have been targeted. On
a case-by-case basis, observers frequently disagree on whether
an individual incident shows definitive evidence of racial
profiling. For example, Lieutenant Steve James, president
of the Long Beach Police Officers Association in California,

insists that his fellow officers never engage in the practice. "There is no racial profiling. There just isn't." He goes on to clarify that "there is criminal profiling,"—the identification of a suspect in a specific crime based on a witness's description of the criminal.

However, most experts conclude that racial profiling is pervasive throughout US society. People of color face a dramatically higher level of suspicion in almost every aspect of their lives, a situation that some call "breathing while black" or "breathing while brown." The ACLU writes that racial profiling "occurs every day, in cities and towns across the country, when law enforcement and private security target people of color for humiliating and often frightening

DEFINITIONS AND DISTINCTIONS

Racial profiling is not the same as criminal profiling. One of the key characteristics of racial profiling is that it typically takes place *before* any crime is known to have been committed or in the absence of evidence that any specific crime has been committed. Criminal profiling, on the other hand, happens *after* a crime takes place. It's a tool law enforcement experts use to narrow the search for a suspect by applying "specific evidence about a particular, known case," as well as by drawing on information about people who have committed similar crimes in the past. Essentially, criminal profiling asks the question, "Who is most likely to have carried out this specific crime?" while racial profiling tends to ask, "Who might commit a crime at some point in the future?" or "Who seems likely to have committed an unknown, unspecified crime?" All the same, both types of profiling typically rely disproportionately on race as an indicator of potential or past criminal behavior.

detentions, interrogations, and searches without evidence of criminal activity and based on perceived race, ethnicity, national origin, or religion. . . . Racial profiling has led countless people to live in fear, casting entire communities as suspect simply because of what they look like, where they come from, or what religion they adhere to."

While racial profiling is closely tied to law enforcement, any institution or individual can engage in profiling. Individuals may profile coworkers, neighbors, and even strangers they encounter in passing. (While individuals often profile people whose backgrounds differ from their own, people may also profile others who share their own racial, ethnic, religious, or national heritage.) Often, however, these individual acts of profiling can be traced to institutions— such as schools, businesses, law enforcement agencies, and government bodies—that allow and even encourage profiling. The structure, rules, and practices of US institutions together foster a larger system of racial bias that stretches far beyond the actions of any single person, leading to widespread racial profiling across all sectors of US society.

Economists, legal scholars, psychologists, and other experts who study racial profiling in the United States stress that the majority of citizens do not deliberately single out or mistreat individuals because of race, ethnicity, or religion. Profiling is often implicit (subtle and frequently unintentional) rather than explicit (intentional and overt). Many people are not consciously aware that they are racially profiling and genuinely believe they have other, valid reasons for suspecting certain people of criminal behavior. Institutions too may have policies that aim to be unbiased yet, in practice, feed a cycle of racial profiling and inequality.

Whether implicit or explicit, individual or institutional, racial profiling leaves deep psychological scars among its victims, hinders the social and economic opportunities of people of color, and creates deep mistrust and fear at all levels of society. Racial profiling in the United States stems from centuries of embedded racism, as well as deeply ingrained modern viewpoints, patterns of discrimination, and privilege.

The Roots of Racial Profiling: Stereotypes, Prejudice, and Racism

Racial profiling in the United States arises from deeply ingrained stereotypes—often unconscious beliefs about the characteristics and behaviors of certain groups of people based on oversimplification and outright inaccuracy. Common stereotypes in the United States are based on a deeply rooted, historical philosophy of racial superiority and include the perceptions that people of color are less honest, less hardworking, and less intelligent than white people. Black people, particularly black males, are often stereotyped as irrational, violent, hypersexualized, and prone to criminal behavior. Latino Americans often encounter assumptions that they are in the nation illegally to work menial jobs or to profit from ties to drug trafficking. Muslims and people of Middle Eastern descent are frequently stereotyped as religious extremists and terrorists.

These stereotypes are rooted in the nation's long history of discriminatory laws—including the legacy of slavery—and are intensified by twenty-first-century flashpoint issues, such as global terrorism and immigration. Family and community traditions, popular culture, media, and personal experience can all shape the stereotypes that people apply to others, especially to those who are somehow different from themselves. Such perceptions can contribute to prejudice and racism. Prejudice is a set of preconceived opinions, based on emotion rather than reason, about the traits and capacities of certain racial groups. Racism is a belief in the superiority of a particular race over others. Both prejudice and racism often exist at an unconscious level, and both are supported by institutional, cultural, legal, and economic practices.

The collective prejudices of individuals within society have influenced laws, business policies, and other institutional practices. Even when the people who created them are no longer involved, these attitudes and practices remain. These practices, in turn, influence the behavior of other individuals and create large-scale systems of racial bias. Fed by stereotyping, prejudice, and racism, racial profiling persists within these society-wide systems.

White Privilege

Racial profiling is intimately linked to white privilege, the institutionalized advantages that white (European American) people encounter in all aspects of American society and that translate into disadvantages for people of color. In particular, European Americans are far less likely than Americans of color to be suspected of criminal behavior—and far less likely to receive harsh treatment if they are arrested for or found guilty of a crime. According to civil rights advocate Jennifer Holladay, "White skin privilege serves several functions. First, it provides white people with 'perks' that [they] do not earn and that people of color do not enjoy. Second, it creates real advantages. . . . White people are immune to a lot of challenges. Finally, white privilege shapes the world in which we live—the way that we navigate and interact with one another and with the world."

In an influential paper, "White Privilege and Male Privilege," women's studies scholar Peggy McIntosh of Wellesley College in Massachusetts identified forty-six ways in which a white person assumes a wide range of unspoken privileges. These include the following:

> 6. *I can turn on the television or open to the front page of the paper and see people of my race widely and positively represented. . . .*
>
> 15. *I did not have to educate our children to be aware of systemic racism for their own daily physical protection. . . .*
>
> 21. *I am never asked to speak for all the people of my racial group. . . .*
>
> 34. *I can worry about racism without being seen as*

self-interested or selfseeking.

41. *I can be sure that if I need legal or medical help, my race will not work against me.*

Not everyone believes that white privilege plays a defining role in American life. Many Americans argue that they have achieved career success, financial security, or other assets through their own abilities and hard work—often in spite of significant hardships, such as poverty or class prejudice. In 2014 and 2015, filmmaker Whitney Dow created the Whiteness Project, a series of interviews with young white people about race and racism. One interviewee, twenty-one-year-old Mackenna, insisted, "Any benefit I've got is because it's something I've worked hard for. . . . If I'm going to be benefiting from something it's because . . . I have a good personality or I worked really hard for it or I'm experienced enough for it."

A study published by the *Journal of Experimental Social Psychology* found that even seeing evidence of their advantages—and the corresponding disadvantages facing nonwhite people—did not convince European Americans of their own race privilege. The study's authors reflected that white people are reluctant to recognize white privilege because they "are motivated to believe that . . . personal virtues determine life outcomes."

Holladay and others contend that while many white individuals certainly do work hard, they also benefit—in sometimes unseen ways—from systems skewed in their favor based on their race, even though white privilege "is not something that white people necessarily do, create or enjoy on purpose." The social-media topic "Criming While

White," which emerged on Twitter in 2014, highlighted everyday white privilege in action. To draw attention to racial double standards in the United States, white Twitter users offered personal stories of committing crimes and facing only mild consequences—or none at all. Sample tweets included "Arrested for DUI, cop took me to drive through ATM so I'd have money to bail myself out" and "Shoplifted when I was a teenager. Was apprehended but never charged because I looked 'like a good kid.'"

Justifications for Racial Profiling

According to the ACLU, "Racial profiling is patently illegal, violating the US Constitution's core promises of equal protection under the law to all and freedom from unreasonable searches and seizures." By contrast, many law enforcement agencies contend that racial profiling can be a valuable crime-fighting tool under certain circumstances. In some cases, profiling defenders argue, members of a certain racial or ethnic group are statistically more likely to engage in a particular kind of criminal behavior, and because police officers have limited time, they need to focus their attention and resources on those groups. For instance, on a federal level, immigration officials contend that a person of Latin American descent is more likely than a white person to be an undocumented immigrant from Mexico. "The immigration investigators have said, 'We can't do our job without taking ethnicity into account. We are very dependent on that,'" says an anonymous official at the Department of Homeland Security (DHS), the federal agency in charge of preventing terrorism, maintaining border security, and overseeing immigration laws.

FBI agents have applied the same reasoning to antiterrorism methods that involve racial profiling. If an agent is investigating a Somali-based militant Islamist group, for example, it would be logical to focus on areas in the United States with large Somali populations. Asra Nomani, a Muslim American journalism professor at Georgetown University in Washington, DC, takes this view. "On issues of safety, profiling means making practical threat assessments," she says. "It's time that we, as a nation, ditch political correctness and choose pragmatism, recognizing that race, religion, and ethnicity can play an important role in criminality."

Some scholars also note that if profiling reduces crime in the targeted community, it can be more helpful than hurtful to residents of color. Ethics expert Mathias Risse and political economist Richard Zeckhauser note how this argument applies to African American communities, pointing out that "historically, much police racism took the form of *under-enforcement*, ignoring black-on-black crime." Theoretically, a more engaged police force will have an overall positive effect on residents' safety, even if the tradeoff is an increase in racial profiling.

Profits of Profiling

For some law enforcement officials, financial gain provides a powerful motivation for engaging in racial profiling. Police departments draw much of their revenue from ticketing, so some officers consider it in their best interest to issue as many tickets as possible. Officers may target people of color for traffic stops, believing these drivers are more likely to live in poverty—and therefore less likely to have automobile insurance, valid driver's licenses, or properly working vehicle features (such as taillights). In profiling people of color, police may also assume that their targets will be unable to afford a lawyer to challenge the ticket in court. Michigan state trooper Craig Tuer alleges that these tactics are encouraged by police department training programs. "The police I do not believe for a minute are inherently racist," Tuer says, "but the policies that are put in place reward a racist behavior."

Police also gain revenue by confiscating and reselling property that they suspect the owner obtained illicitly. Cash, automobiles, and even homes can be seized by officers without proof of the owner's wrongdoing. The money from property sales often goes toward departments' operational costs, including officers' salaries—giving individual police officers a powerful incentive to conduct seizures. Advocacy groups such as the ACLU argue that officers target people of color because they believe those individuals will be less likely to have the resources to challenge a seizure.

Arrests for drug-related offenses can be equally profitable for police departments. The federal government provides funding to state and local law enforcement agencies based partially on how many drug arrests they make. Civil rights advocate and Ohio State University law professor Michelle Alexander says that this results in police "stopping, frisking, searching as many people as possible, pulling over as many cars as possible, in order to boost their numbers up and ensure the funding stream will continue or increase." The main targets are people of color, whom police and the public perceive to be more likely to use drugs. Police department supervisors often put pressure on officers to make a certain number of arrests each month or year. "It's a numbers game," says Julio Valentin, a retired New York police officer and a professor at John Jay College of Criminal Justice in New York. "Commanders are trying to be proactive, or show that they're being proactive, and here they have a system where [officers] are told, 'Get those numbers [of stops and arrests] to where they should be and you'll get your promotion.'"

Results of Racial Profiling

Numerous studies indicate that profiling based on race, religion, or ethnicity fails to deter crime in any significant way. In part, this is because law enforcement officials are acting on fundamentally flawed assumptions, such as the idea that black and Latino Americans commit more drug offenses than white citizens. Extensive studies by universities, government agencies, and independent research organizations have shown that people of color commit nonviolent crimes—such as traffic violations, drug-related offenses, and possession of weapons—at essentially the same rate as white people. Thus, profiling people of color as likely suspects in these types of crimes is generally ineffective.

In fact, some experts argue that when law enforcement agencies focus on race and ethnicity, they miss opportunities to track criminal behavior more efficiently. As University of Pittsburgh law professor David A. Harris notes, "If you want to know if somebody is involved in, say, transporting drugs on a highway, if you want to know whether somebody might be up to no good in an airport, you should watch with unrelenting intensity what they are doing, not what they look like—because that's the only good predictor."

Racial profiling also negatively affects crime prevention by undermining citizens' trust in law enforcement. People of color are more likely than white people to view the US criminal justice system as unfair. A 2015 poll commissioned by the National Bar Association (an organization of attorneys) found that 88 percent of black Americans—compared to 59 percent of white Americans—believe police treat them unfairly. The perception that a police force is biased against people of color can create an atmosphere of tension, fear, and hostility, particularly in communities of color with high rates of crime. And racial profiling incidents leave lingering psychological scars on those who are targeted, deepening this sense of mistrust. As a result, residents may become unwilling to cooperate with law enforcement officers in solving crimes and in working toward common goals of safer and more peaceful communities. This sense of alienation can apply not only to local and state police departments but to US government agencies such as the Department of Homeland Security. Somali American activist Jaylani Hussein explains why many Muslim Americans, including Somalis, find it difficult to

Ilhan Omar *(right)*, a Muslim American born in Somalia, ran for the Minnesota House of Representatives in 2016. Her campaign platform included calls for police reform, criminal justice reform, and other measures to combat institutional racism. She emphasized the need for law enforcement to work cooperatively and build trust with community members.

work constructively with federal agencies. "They want Somali leaders to be a part of task forces and have conversations about countering extremism, but they treat everyone like a suspect."

The ACLU concludes, "Racial profiling is ineffective. It alienates communities from law enforcement, hinders community policing efforts, and causes law enforcement to lose credibility and trust among the people they are sworn to protect and serve." In the minds of many Americans, the United States' entire criminal justice system—and indeed the very fabric of society—is tainted by racial discrimination. While racial profiling is not the sole cause of this disillusionment, it is both a product of and a contributor to larger issues of American racial injustice.

A young man drinks from a segregated water fountain—an everyday example of racial segregation in the American South prior to civil rights legislation of the 1960s.

CHAPTER 2
HISTORIC INEQUALITY

In 1846 former slave, social reformer, and abolitionist Frederick Douglass left the United States for the first time. During a speaking tour in Great Britain, he was amazed to discover how little prejudice he encountered. "There is no distinction on account of color," he wrote to a friend back in the United States. "The white man gains nothing by being white, and the black man loses nothing by being black." When he went to public gardens, museums, and theaters, he noticed that white people "looked as though they thought I had as much right [to be] there as themselves." This was a new experience for Douglass. In the United States, he was accustomed to being "carefully excluded" because of his race. Born into slavery—from which he eventually escaped—he had spent his entire life struggling against discrimination. His time in Great Britain reinforced what he already knew: race relations in the United States are tied to the country's distinct, complex history of slavery and racially discriminatory laws.

More than 120 years after Douglass's death, twenty-first-century Americans still grapple with racial tensions, misunderstandings, and injustices. Racial profiling in the modern United States stems from these issues, which stretch back centuries.

Diversity and Conflict

The United States is an ethnically, culturally, and religiously diverse nation, and that diversity dates back

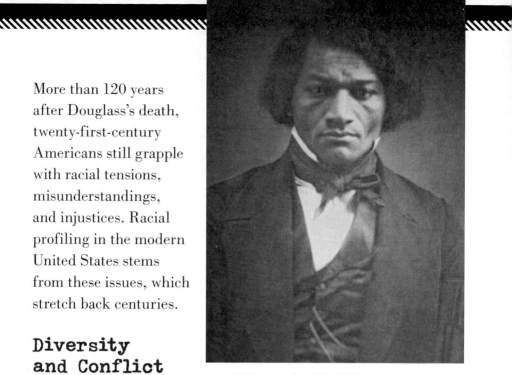

Frederick Douglass (ca. 1818–1895) was born into slavery in Maryland, escaped to the North as a young man, and became an outspoken opponent of slavery and advocate of equality. As an author and public speaker, he called attention to the entrenched discrimination he and other people of color faced in the United States.

to the country's origins. North America's first inhabitants were numerous distinct indigenous peoples with their own cultures, faiths, and governing systems. By the early seventeenth century, large numbers of European adventurers and settlers—most of whom were white Christians—had begun arriving on the continent. European colonizers sought to push the original inhabitants off the land and to impose their own customs on indigenous populations, often through violence. In the centuries that followed, American Indians suffered genocidal losses through colonial and US military conquest and through government policies of eradication, including forced relocation to reservations.

After European settlers arrived in North America, slave traders began bringing West African captives to the continent. Along with enslaved indigenous Americans, these enslaved Africans were legally the property of their white masters. Slavery became entrenched in the American South, where the economy depended on plantations that produced cotton, tobacco, and rice for sale domestically and overseas. To maintain the large-scale production of these crops, plantation owners relied on the free labor of enslaved workers. Besides tending crops, slaves ran white colonists' households, where they cooked, cleaned, sewed, raised children, and cared for all the needs of their masters' families. Slave owners often forced captives to work under brutal conditions, with no personal privacy or protection from violence. White masters routinely raped enslaved women and girls. Owners had the legal right to abuse and even kill slaves.

Enslaved people had no legal rights. Colonial laws generally barred slaves from owning property, legally marrying, testifying in court, voting, and learning to read. At slave auctions, family members could be sold, separating parents from children and husbands from wives. For the vast majority of enslaved people, escape was impossible. Colonial police patrols (also known as slave patrols) were formed specifically to monitor slaves' movements, pursuing and capturing those who attempted to run away. White people who aided in the capture of runaway slaves received monetary rewards—a further economic incentive to support the institution of slavery. Recaptured fugitives were usually returned to their owners and subjected to brutal punishments.

During this time, stereotypes about people of African descent became institutionalized among white colonists. Through propaganda that ranged from newspaper articles to religious sermons, supporters of slavery spread false ideas

Before states in the South had organized police forces, slave patrols tracked the movements and activities of people of color. Patrollers and professional slave catchers captured runaway slaves and returned them to their owners. Slave catchers often pursued fugitives into the North, where they also kidnapped free black people and sold them into slavery. This 1839 illustration from *The Anti-Slavery Almanac* shows white northerners kidnapping a free black man, likely with the intention of handing him over to slave catchers from the South.

that black people were less intelligent, less hardworking, and more prone to violence than white people. In particular, many colonists portrayed black men as physically threatening to white men and sexually threatening to white women. These stereotypes—used to justify slavery—would persist for centuries, despite having no basis in fact.

After the United States won independence from Great Britain in the Revolutionary War (1775–1783), a growing number of northern states abolished slavery—largely because their economies were based on manufacturing, not agriculture, and depended on paid (largely immigrant) labor instead of unpaid slave labor. The framers of the US Constitution—ratified in 1788—were keenly aware of racial tensions and oppression within the new United States. Yet they chose not to outlaw slavery or extend the rights of citizenship to nonwhite Americans, believing leaders could address these issues later.

Throughout the young nation, enslaved peoples and their allies fought for the end of slavery. Many slaves sought safety and freedom in the northern United States and in Canada, where slavery had been abolished. By the mid-nineteenth century, private citizens had established a network of safe houses and secret routes to the North, known as the Underground Railroad. Aided by black, white, and American Indian opponents of slavery, hundreds of runaway slaves used these routes to reach freedom. But law enforcement officials and professional slave catchers had the legal right to capture runaways and return them to slavery—or kill them. The few fugitives who did reach the North struggled against pervasive prejudice there and faced limited opportunities for employment, housing, and education.

Disagreements about whether slavery should remain legal fueled deepening tensions among the nation's states. These tensions eventually sparked the American Civil War (1861–1865). Eleven slaveholding states in the South chose to break away from the United States (the Union) to form a new nation, the Confederate States of America, where slavery would remain legal. At the war's outset, the primary goal of US president Abraham Lincoln was to preserve a unified nation. He eventually became convinced that the issues dividing the states would never be resolved while slavery continued. Shortly after the war ended, with a Union victory, slavery was formally outlawed throughout the United States with the ratification of the Thirteenth Amendment to the US Constitution in December 1865.

Legacies of Violence

After the Civil War and the abolition of slavery, the US government pursued a policy known as Reconstruction, which aimed to bring the southern states back into the Union and to promote the legal rights of black people in the South. Former Confederate states were required to accept the Fourteenth

Amendment to the US Constitution, which the US Congress ratified in 1868. This amendment officially granted citizenship to black Americans, giving black men the right to vote and entitling all black people to "equal protection of the laws." Many white southerners resisted these changes.

The right of black men to vote became a primary target of opposition. The Fifteenth Amendment to the US Constitution, ratified in 1870, declared that states could not legally ban African American men from voting. However, lawmakers in the South found ways to work around this regulation. One strategy was to establish literacy tests as a requirement for voter registration. Because learning to read had been illegal for enslaved Americans, many black southerners were illiterate. To target black men who *could* read, state legislatures passed laws that allowed voting registration officials to tailor literacy tests. This flexibility meant that an official could ask a white voter to read and answer a single, simple question, virtually guaranteeing that he would pass, while presenting a long series of complex questions to a black voter and allowing him to register only if he got every answer right. Another tactic was instituting poll taxes—voter registration fees. Many African Americans (as well as some white citizens) in the South could not afford these fees.

Exclusion of African Americans extended beyond the ballot box into daily life. Millions of newly freed African Americans struggled to find work and to buy property. In the rural South, black families rented small plots of land and farming equipment from white landowners in return for a large portion of their yearly crop. This system, called sharecropping, was designed to keep laborers in constant debt to their landlords, locking many black Americans into a system of unpaid work and often insurmountable poverty.

Sharecropping, a system in which poor black and white families rented small plots of farmland from wealthy white owners, locked many southern black families in a cycle of debt and poverty for generations. This family was photographed working in a Georgia cotton field in 1941.

Beginning in the 1870s, many southern states passed laws mandating segregation—the separation of black and white Americans in public spaces. Known as Jim Crow laws, these policies were especially common in former slaveholding states. Depending on the individual state, white people and black people were legally required to use separate movie theaters, restaurants, hospitals, restrooms, water fountains, prisons, train cars, buses, hotels, schools, libraries, and cemeteries. Supporters of segregation often described segregated facilities as "separate but equal." Opponents argued that in practice, black institutions and facilities received less funding and had less access to resources than white institutions—disadvantages that fueled social and economic inequalities. Moreover, segregation sent the message that people of color were unworthy of sharing spaces with white people. Charles Hamilton Houston, a Washington, DC, lawyer who worked to end segregation during the 1930s, 1940s, and 1950s, insisted, "There is no such thing as separate but equal. Segregation itself imports [signifies] inequality."

Law enforcement institutions also actively participated in the marginalization of black Americans. Legislators throughout the South passed laws designed to heavily penalize black citizens for minor crimes. In fact, many of these laws invented punishable crimes, such as changing jobs without a previous employer's permission or being unable to produce proof of employment when stopped by a law enforcement officer. According to Pulitzer Prize-winning journalist and author Douglas Blackmon, such laws were "designed to criminalize black life—to make it essentially impossible for any African American man . . . to not be in violation of some law at almost all times." Although the laws did not explicitly apply only to African Americans, "overwhelmingly, they were only ever enforced against African Americans."

Between the 1860s and the 1940s, thousands of black people were arrested under these laws and sentenced to months or years of hard labor in a practice called convict leasing. Local businesses, as well as large companies based in both the South and the North, paid law enforcement agencies for the labor of black convicts, creating a widespread, profitable system of labor that echoed the institution of slavery. For black prisoners caught in the physically grueling, psychologically devastating, and often deadly work of convict leasing, civic engagement was impossible. For the rest of the black population, the risk of arrest due to the color of their skin hung over them as they walked to work, as they made long treks to the nearest schools, and as they approached polling places on election days.

The justice system was not the only institution that posed deadly threats to black Americans. In the South and elsewhere, private citizens also targeted black Americans. For example, white Americans opposed to racial equality formed unofficial groups, sometimes called vigilance committees, to promote the protection of white citizens. In reality, these groups aimed to intimidate black Americans so they would not exercise their legal rights. The most infamous and formalized of these groups was the Ku Klux Klan (KKK), which was originally formed in 1865 by former Confederate soldiers who opposed Reconstruction. KKK members sabotaged, harassed, and killed African Americans, as well as some white citizens who supported the rights of black Americans. The KKK and other civilian groups used multiple tactics against their targets, including burning African American churches and schools.

The most extreme form of civilian violence against black Americans was lynching. This form of mob punishment occurred outside the legal process. Perpetrators typically murdered victims by hanging or shooting, often after inflicting physical abuse and torture. Private citizens spearheaded lynchings in response to alleged crimes, especially alleged sexual transgressions by black men and boys against white women and girls. Mob participants, many of whom were leading members of society, rarely faced social or legal repercussions for these killings. Lynching peaked in the 1880s and early 1890s, especially—but not exclusively—in southern US states. "Our country's national crime is lynching," Ida B. Wells, a black journalist and antilynching activist, wrote in 1900. "It represents the cool, calculating deliberation of intelligent people who openly avow that there is an 'unwritten law' that justifies them in putting human beings to death without complaint under oath, without trial by jury, without opportunity to make defense, and without right of appeal."

The exact number of lynching victims may never be known. A 2015 study by the Equal Justice Initiative, a legal

Members of the Ku Klux Klan regularly burned crosses on the property of people they targeted for intimidation. Well beyond the nineteenth century, black citizens, as well as some white citizens who opposed the KKK, endured open threats of violence from the KKK and other white-supremacist vigilantes.

advocacy organization, reported that nearly four thousand African Americans were lynched in just twelve southern states between 1877 and 1950. The report's authors wrote, "Lynchings were violent and public acts of torture that traumatized black people throughout the country and were largely tolerated by state and federal officials. These lynchings were terrorism."

With a long history of terrorizing black Americans, especially in the South, law enforcement agencies and the legal system largely gave their unspoken approval to the brutality of lynching. Some law enforcement officers and private citizens did intervene to prevent individual lynchings, but law enforcement agencies took no action to address the practice at large. This type of institutional inaction is another form of racial profiling. In fact, the ACLU includes "discriminatory omissions on the part of law enforcement" in its definition of racial profiling.

Beyond Black and White

Black Americans were not the only targets of racial bias and profiling after the Civil War. Throughout the nineteenth century, large numbers of immigrants came to the United States from all over the world, fleeing poverty, war, religious persecution, and other hardships. They moved to the United States seeking better lives and greater opportunities for themselves and their families. When they arrived, they faced deep-seated prejudice against foreigners. New immigrants spoke many different languages and followed religions, dress styles, and customs that were unfamiliar to mainstream Americans. And many simply looked different from their white European American neighbors. These differences often led to tension with fellow Americans, especially with poor white Americans who feared losing their low-paying jobs to new immigrants willing to work for even lower wages. At various times, immigrants from European countries—such as Ireland, Poland, and Sweden—faced suspicion and discrimination.

The most extreme and sustained prejudice generally fell on non-European immigrants. For example, in the early to mid nineteenth century, many Chinese immigrants arrived in the United States. Some of them helped build the first transcontinental railroad, which linked the eastern United States with the West and was completed in 1869. Many white Americans regarded the newcomers with hostility, and Chinese immigrants experienced widespread discrimination that sometimes erupted in violence. In October 1871, for example, hundreds of white Americans entered Chinatown in Los Angeles and attacked residents, killing at least eighteen immigrants. Eventually, anti-Chinese sentiment led to the Chinese Exclusion Act of 1882, a federal law that ended immigration from China for the next several decades.

Still seeking a steady supply of cheap labor, US industries turned to Japanese immigrants, whose arrival provoked the same prejudices and suspicions as their Chinese predecessors. In San Francisco, California, for instance, a 1906 school board decision segregated the city's public schools, requiring white children and children of Asian descent to attend separate schools. By 1908 the US government had severely limited the number of Japanese workers who could enter the country, and US employers began relying on Mexican workers to fill their need for cheap labor.

Mexican immigrants fled political and economic instability in their native country and took low-paying jobs in the US agricultural, mining, construction, and transportation industries, sparking resentment from white workers who held the same jobs. That resentment grew during the Great Depression (1929–1942), a serious, global economic downturn. In the United States, millions of people lost their jobs and homes. In response, US leaders decided to deport some Mexican workers so that their jobs would be available for white citizens. During the 1930s, the US government forced hundreds of thousands of Mexican immigrants and Mexican American citizens to leave the country. Yet when the United States entered World War II (1939–1945) and thousands of white American men enlisted in the armed forces, US employers sought Mexican workers to fill the new labor shortage.

"POTENTIAL ENEMIES OF JAPANESE EXTRACTION"

In 1941, following a Japanese attack on the US naval base at Pearl Harbor, Hawaii, the United States declared war on Japan and entered World War II. Early the next year, with President Franklin Roosevelt's authorization in Executive Order 9066, more than one hundred thousand Japanese Americans—many of whom had been born in the United States—were forced to leave their homes and move to remote internment camps in the western United States. The US government claimed that the forced relocation was for the safety of these citizens, who did face suspicion and hostility from some Americans during the war. However, as one Japanese American imprisoned in a camp noted later, "If we were put there for our protection, why were the guns at the guard towers pointed inward, instead of outward?"

In reality, Roosevelt's policy was a case of government-sanctioned racial profiling. It arose largely out of prejudice against Japanese Americans and a fear that they might act as spies—even though officials had no evidence of any such activity. A 1942 report by a US military commander, recommending the relocation and imprisonment policy, made its aims clear: "The Japanese race is an enemy race and while many second and third generation Japanese born on United States soil, possessed of United States citizenship, have become 'Americanized,' the racial strains are undiluted. . . . It therefore follows that along the vital Pacific Coast over 112,000 potential enemies of Japanese extraction are at large today."

In May 1945, this Japanese American family returned to Seattle, Washington, after being confined in an Idaho internment camp. They discovered that neighbors had vandalized their home during their absence, breaking windows and covering the house and garage with anti-Japanese graffiti.

A 1942 agreement between the US and Mexican governments allowed Mexican citizens to enter the United States and contract with US companies as guest workers. After the war, this labor program continued, and US industries became increasingly dependent on Mexican manual labor. Employers hired both authorized workers who came through the labor program and Mexicans who entered the United States unofficially. As a result, illegal immigration to the United States from Mexico spiked during the 1950s and 1960s. Although the US government officially ended the labor program in 1964, American industries' reliance on cheap Mexican labor continued. So did widespread stereotyping of Mexicans and others of Latin American descent.

Economic Inequality

Well into the twentieth century, white Americans—from legislators to journalists to scholars—continued to portray African Americans as more violent, less hardworking, and less intelligent than white people. To mask the devastating effects of racist policies, white supremacists claimed African Americans were naturally incapable of earning a living or being financially responsible. These myths, in turn, helped launch a new wave of racially biased economic policies and a particular kind of racial profiling known as redlining.

To help the American economy recover from the economic blows of the Great Depression, the US government made it easier for Americans to afford to buy homes. The Home Owners' Loan Corporation (HOLC), established by the federal government in 1933, granted home loans, or mortgages, that were insured by the Federal Housing Administration (FHA), a government agency created in 1934. Between the mid-1930s and the early 1960s, the US government backed $120 billion of home loans, 98 percent of which went to white borrowers. In fact, the official policy of HOLC and the FHA identified people of color, regardless of their social class, as financial risks who should not receive government loans.

The two agencies created color-coded city maps that categorized neighborhoods by their perceived financial risk level. Areas occupied by people of color, specifically black and Latino Americans, were marked in red. Known as redlining, this practice of denying loans to people of color spread beyond the federal government to private mortgage companies throughout the country. As journalist Jamelle Bouie writes, "These institutions, private and public, didn't *cause* racism in housing markets, but they gave it official sanction [approval], which—over time—influenced how individuals understood the value of their homes and neighborhoods. A white neighborhood was a good one; a black neighborhood, a bad one."

The racial bias in the mortgage market led to a type of unofficial yet institutionalized segregation across the United States. Many white families moved into relatively affluent, safe suburbs, especially as the US economy rebounded following World War II. Most families of color, meanwhile, lived in inner cities, where predatory landlords rented out poorly maintained homes at inflated prices.

A home is a valuable asset that increases the owner's net worth (financial holdings), since the owner can theoretically sell it one day for a profit. White home buyers were dramatically increasing their net worth with purchases of brand-new suburban homes. Yet the vast majority of people of color were forced to rent low-grade inner-city housing. Renting

Redlining Codes

Wealthy white, generally Protestant residents

Middle-class Americans of Jewish, Irish, and Italian descent

Working-class white people

People of color

This map shows how government workers coded the city of Oakland, California, in 1937. The federal government and private mortgage companies avoided granting loans to residents of "red" neighborhoods populated by people of color. "Orange" neighborhoods were considered less undesirable but still at risk of "infiltration" by people of color. "Blue" and especially "green" areas were seen as good investments for lenders.

does not increase the net worth of the family who is paying the rent, only that of the property's owner. The FHA's portrayal of "red" neighborhoods as undesirable places to live became a self-fulfilling prophecy. With neither government agencies nor private companies willing to invest in "red" neighborhoods, these areas suffered from a lack of infrastructure (facilities and resources). This contributed to widespread poverty—and to the high crime rates that stem from poverty. Police forces tended to target these areas far more heavily than largely white suburban communities, reinforcing white Americans' association of people of color with crime and violence.

CASE STUDY: EMMETT TILL

In the summer of 1955, fourteen-year-old Emmett Till *(below)*, who lived in Chicago, Illinois, was visiting relatives in Money, Mississippi. On August 24, Till bought gum at a local grocery store owned by a white couple, Roy and Carolyn Bryant. According to local teens, Till briefly talked to and perhaps whistled at Carolyn Bryant. In the deeply segregated South, attention from a black male toward a white woman could bring grave consequences. Early on August 28, Roy Bryant and his half brother, J. W. Milam, kidnapped Till, beat him severely, shot him in the head, and rolled his body into the river. Bryant and Milam were arrested the next day. Till's body was found downstream several days later.

Thousands of people attended Till's funeral in Chicago on September 3. Till's mother chose to leave the casket open, revealing the boy's gruesome injuries. Historian Robin Kelley credits newspaper images of the body with exposing "the level of violence that was commonplace in a place like Mississippi" and inspiring more people to speak out against Jim Crow. Back in Mississippi, the trial of Bryant and Milam lasted just five days. The all-white jury acquitted Bryant and Milam of Till's murder on September 23, 1955. A few months later, *Look* magazine published an exclusive interview with Milam in which Milam confirmed that he and Bryant had murdered Till. As he spoke of the killing, Milam revealed that he had been motivated by a general desire to keep black people "in their place." He was also determined that African Americans "ain't gonna vote where I live. If they did, they'd control the government. They ain't gonna go to school with my kids." Because the men had already been tried for the murder, they could not be tried again, despite this open acknowledgment of guilt. Americans reacted with renewed grief and shock. Till became a potent symbol of the need for racial equality and justice. Mississippi has since created a historical trail to show how events such as the Till murder helped launch the modern civil rights movement.

Building a Movement

In the 1950s, black activists in the United States began drawing national attention with coordinated efforts to promote equal rights for African Americans. The civil rights movement, as this wave of activism came to be called, waged its struggle on two fronts: first, advocating for laws against institutionalized racial bias and, second, working to put those laws into practice in communities where discrimination remained rampant.

In May 1954, a major US Supreme Court case marked an early victory for the civil rights movement and an important step toward ending segregation. In *Brown v. Board of Education*, the court ruled unanimously that state laws enforcing the segregation of black students and white students in separate public schools were unconstitutional. In practice, desegregation of public schools in the South did not begin until 1960. Black citizens who spearheaded the integration of schools throughout the nation faced continuing opposition. Many white citizens withdrew their children from integrated schools and harassed black students. Opponents of integration routinely invoked ugly stereotypes about black people's inferior intelligence and even inferior hygiene as justification for racial segregation.

During the 1950s and 1960s, civil rights activists also worked to desegregate public transportation, lunch counters and restaurants, housing, and numerous other public places and private businesses. The response from white citizens— as well as local, state, and national institutions—was often hostile. Police arrested civil rights activists for carrying out peaceful demonstrations. On several occasions, police officers attacked demonstrators with tear gas, clubs, and vicious police dogs. Segregationists bombed black churches, businesses, and homes—acts of terrorism that law enforcement rarely investigated. In Birmingham, Alabama, for instance, more than fifty unsolved bombings ravaged black neighborhoods between 1947 and 1965. After one such attack, a 1963 church bombing that killed four African American girls, white Birmingham lawyer Charles Morgan Jr. accused the police force of failing black citizens: "There are no Negro policemen; there are no Negro sheriff's deputies. . . . Do not misunderstand me. It is not that I think that white policemen had anything whatsoever to do with the killing of these children or previous bombings. It's just that Negroes who see an all-white police force must think in terms of its failure to prevent or solve the bombing and think perhaps Negroes would have worked a little harder."

At the federal level too, the movement had enemies in the highest ranks of law enforcement. J. Edgar Hoover, who served as the director of the FBI from 1924 to 1972, viewed the civil rights movement as a threat to national security. Hoover placed leading civil rights activists such as Martin Luther King Jr. under surveillance and instructed agents not to intervene when they witnessed violence against civil rights activists.

Some of the civil rights movement's most vocal opponents were political leaders, especially in southern states. On January 14, 1963, George Wallace—the newly elected governor of Alabama—inspired thunderous applause from his audience when he addressed the issue in his inaugural speech: "I say, segregation now, segregation tomorrow and segregation forever."

The pressure for change and racial justice was enormous. Despite widespread opposition to civil rights legislation, the US Congress passed the Civil Rights Act, which President Lyndon Johnson signed into law in July 1964. This landmark

In August 1963, hundreds of thousands of civil rights advocates gathered for the historic March on Washington for Jobs and Freedom in Washington, DC. Martin Luther King Jr. *(front, far left)* was among the prominent civil rights leaders who organized and spoke at the march.

law prohibited discrimination based on race, color, religion, sex, or national origin. The Voting Rights Act of 1965, also signed into law by President Johnson, prohibited racially discriminatory barriers to voting such as literacy tests and poll taxes. The US Supreme Court legalized interracial marriage across the nation in 1967, and the Fair Housing Act of 1968 outlawed redlining. (Nonetheless, the mortgage industry has unofficially continued to implement similar practices.)

Dissent and Disruption

Despite its significant victories, the civil rights movement encountered powerful resistance and suffered numerous setbacks. Prominent black activists and white allies of the movement were assassinated. These included President John F. Kennedy in 1963, activist Malcolm X in 1965, activist Martin Luther King Jr. in 1968, and New York senator Robert F. Kennedy in 1968.

PROFILE OF A MARRIAGE

On the morning of July 11, 1958, newlyweds Richard and Mildred Loving *(shown below in 1965)* were asleep at their house in Central Point, Virginia, when the county sheriff and two deputies burst into their bedroom. One of the officers asked Richard, "Who is this woman you're sleeping with?" Mildred said, "I'm his wife," and Richard showed the officers the Lovings' marriage certificate. The sheriff replied, "That's no good here."

The couple had married five weeks earlier in Washington, DC. Because Richard was white and Mildred was black, the State of Virginia did not recognize their marriage as legal. Virginia was one of twenty-four US states with laws prohibiting interracial marriage. The county sheriff and his deputies had received an anonymous tip that Richard and Mildred had defied the law.

The Lovings were arrested, tried, and sentenced to a year in prison, unless they agreed to leave Virginia for twenty-five years. They chose to move out of the state and a few years later, they challenged the law in court. In 1967 their case—*Loving v. Virginia*—reached the US Supreme Court. The court ruled unanimously in favor of the Lovings, declaring that state bans on interracial marriages are unconstitutional. Richard and Mildred Loving then returned to their home in Virginia to raise their family.

Efforts to desegregate suburban neighborhoods in the North sparked riots, fire bombings, and other acts of violence by white residents. In general, communities and individuals of color received little support from government or law enforcement bodies when they tried to exercise their expanded legal rights.

Long-simmering discontent and animosity over racial inequality sometimes boiled over into violent unrest. For example, in 1965, riots took place in Watts, a mostly black neighborhood of south central Los Angeles, after a white California Highway Patrol officer pulled over a black motorist on suspicion of drunk driving. A crowd soon gathered, and an altercation broke out. In the ensuing six days of riots, thirty-four people died, about one thousand were injured, and nearly four thousand were arrested. Two years later, in July 1967, Detroit, Michigan, was the scene of race riots that left forty-three people dead. In both cases, black residents of these racially divided cities were frustrated and angry about unemployment, discrimination, poverty, and police brutality and prejudice—including racial profiling of black individuals. Similar displays of outrage broke out in cities across the nation including Baltimore, Maryland; Minneapolis, Minnesota; New York City; and Portland, Oregon. Some Americans regarded these incidents as justified uprisings that were part of the ongoing fight for equality, while others viewed them as inexcusable criminal actions.

By the late 1960s, a more radical form of activism emerged in response to the nation's slow progress toward racial equality. In 1966 in Oakland, California, college students Huey P. Newton and Bobby Seale founded the Black Panther Party. This activist group called for an end to racially motivated police brutality, incarceration of black Americans, and racial disparities in employment, housing, and education. By 1969 the Black Panthers had risen to national prominence. Besides calling for black civilians to engage in armed self-defense, the group ran community service ventures that provided free meals for children, health-care services, and educational programs in poor black neighborhoods around the country. The group's militant philosophy and successful organizing of black youth attracted the attention of the FBI, which worked to disrupt the Black Panthers' operations. Over the 1960s and 1970s, the FBI carried out surveillance, intimidation, and murder of activists and their families, planted FBI informants in the movement's ranks, and arrested numerous members on

VOICES OF EXPERIENCE

"I don't know what most white people in this country feel, but I can only conclude what they feel from the state of their institutions. I don't know if white Christians hate Negroes or not, but I know that we have a Christian church which is white and a Christian church which is black. . . . I don't know whether the labor unions and their bosses really hate me. That doesn't matter. But I know that I'm not in their unions. I don't know if the real estate lobby has anything against black people, but I know the real estate lobby keeps me in the ghetto. I don't know if the board of education hates black people, but I know the textbooks they give my children to read and the schools that we go to. Now this is the evidence! You want me to make an act of faith risking myself, my wife . . . my children on some idealism which you assure me exists in America which I have never seen."

—James Baldwin (1924–1987), gay African American author, speaking on the popular *Dick Cavett Show*, 1968 charges that courts frequently found to be unsubstantiated. Police departments also targeted Black Panther activists. The heavy law enforcement scrutiny and violence drove many black Americans away from the group. Escalating violence between Panthers and law enforcement, along with negative media coverage, turned white public opinion against the organization. Plagued by internal strife and concerted law enforcement efforts to squelch the movement, the Black Panther Party floundered in the 1970s and ultimately dissolved in 1982.

The War on Drugs

In the 1970s, a new federal drug policy further targeted communities of color. In response to a nationwide spike in the abuse of recreational drugs such as marijuana, heroin, and cocaine, President Richard Nixon declared a war on drugs aimed at discouraging drug use and disrupting drug trafficking. With support from the Nixon administration, the US Congress passed a series of laws that tightened drug regulations. The Comprehensive Drug Abuse Prevention and Control Act of 1970 allowed law enforcement officers to enter private homes unannounced and search for drugs. "No-knock" searches had far-reaching effects on US communities, particularly communities of color, where the practice quickly became especially common.

John Ehrlichman, Nixon's domestic policy adviser, reportedly admitted in an unpublished 1994 interview that the Nixon administration used the war on drugs to undermine Americans who were critical of the Republican president. Black Americans, who generally support Democratic politicians, were among the main targets. "We knew we couldn't make it illegal to be . . . black, but by getting the public to associate . . . the blacks with heroin, and then criminalizing [heroin] heavily, we could disrupt those communities," Ehrlichman explained. "We could arrest their leaders, raid their homes, break up their meetings, and vilify them night after night on the evening news."

Under Republican president Ronald Reagan, who took office in 1981, the federal government intensified its focus on criminalizing drug use. This was partly in response to a nationwide cocaine crisis that hit urban communities of color especially hard. The Anti-Drug Abuse Act of 1986 created mandatory minimum penalties for drug offenses, meaning that possession of even a tiny amount of a controlled substance carried a prison sentence of several years. Critics of the harsh drug policies alleged that these measures were calculated to target people of color and to appeal to white voters who feared African Americans. Attorney Eric Sterling, who served as the legal counsel to the US House of Representatives committee that drafted the law, later became a critic of the policy. According to Sterling, "The Department of Justice was supposed to be focusing on high-level [drug] traffickers. . . . [Instead] the federal government is looking at insignificant local cases and handing out long sentences to defendants that are predominantly black or Hispanic."

At this time, white Americans were about 45 percent more likely than black Americans to sell cocaine and other drugs. Yet in the following decades, arrests of Americans of color for drug-related crimes skyrocketed, and the swelling populations of American prisons held a disproportionate number of black, Latino, and American Indian inmates. Under the umbrella of the war on drugs, police presence in communities of color continued to intensify. Media outlets routinely linked people of color with criminal behavior, and public servants and private citizens became increasingly likely to make the same association.

Interactions with police were often traumatizing for families of color. Lori Penner, of the Cheyenne and Sac and Fox American Indian nations, remembers the first time local law enforcement searched her home for drugs. "My door was broken down [by police officers]. They pointed guns at us and told us to get on the floor. . . . My 15-year-old daughter was jerked out of the shower and forced to stand naked in front of three male officers. She . . . had to get dressed in front of three officers. . . . The police laughed and smirked at us when no drugs were found. One police officer had the audacity to tell my daughter she cleaned up nice and looks good for a 15-year-old girl."

Profiling and Immigration

Throughout the second half of the twentieth century, political and economic instability in Mexico and many Central and South American countries prompted hundreds of thousands of people from those regions to seek safety and better opportunities for their families in the United States. Some came legally after successfully applying for green cards (permanent resident status with the legal right to seek and accept employment). However, partly due to the limited number of available green cards, the strict qualifications that applicants must meet, and the long waiting period, many Latino immigrants entered the country without legal documentation. Nevertheless, numerous US industries, from agriculture to hospitality (restaurants and hotels) to meatpacking, hired large numbers of Latino workers—typically at very low wages and with few benefits—without concern for legal status.

CASE STUDY: RODNEY KING

On March 3, 1991, Rodney King, a twenty-five-year-old black man, noticed a police cruiser following his car on the streets of Los Angeles, California. King—who had previously spent time in prison for robbery—had been drinking, which was in violation of his parole. He was afraid that if the officers stopped him, he would be arrested and sent back to prison. So he sped away, trying to flee the police. When he eventually did pull over, four white male officers forced King to lie down beside the car, beat him with their batons, and shocked him with a Taser. Seventeen additional officers on the scene observed the beating without intervening. King sustained multiple bone fractures and other injuries that required five hours of surgery.

An observer videotaped the incident and shared the recording with a local news station. Soon the footage was broadcast around the country. In response, Los Angeles County district attorney Ira Reiner charged the four officers who had been directly involved in the beating with "assault with a deadly weapon and excessive use of force by a police officer." However, Reiner chose not to file charges against the seventeen other officers who had been on the scene.

Critics had long accused the Los Angeles Police Department (LAPD) of racial bias and excessive force, sanctioned by Chief Daryl Gates. And the officers' trials did little to bolster black Angelenos' faith in the justice system. The judge decided to hold the trial in Ventura County, a largely white area of Southern California. The jury, chosen from Ventura County residents, consisted of ten white jurors, one Latino juror, and one Asian American juror, all of whom expressed positive views toward law enforcement during jury selection.

The officers' defense lawyers portrayed King as physically imposing and threatening. They made unsubstantiated claims that he had been under the influence of the hallucinogenic drug PCP (phencyclidine) and insisted that King's actions were ultimately to blame for the officers' show of force. "How much force is needed to subdue this unruly, PCP-crazed giant?" the defense lawyers wrote, evoking a centuries-old image of a violent, uncontrollable black man. Several jurors later expressed similar views, telling reporters that King had provoked the beating because he had not sufficiently cooperated with police. After a week of deliberation, the jury acquitted three of the officers and declared a mistrial in the case of the fourth.

LA mayor Tom Bradley spoke out against the decision, saying, "Today that jury asked us to accept the senseless and brutal beating of a helpless man." Almost immediately, protests and rioting broke out across Los Angeles, and black Angelenos took up the rallying cry "No justice, no peace," which echoed across the city. The unrest in LA raged for five days, killing more than fifty people, injuring hundreds more, and causing an estimated $1 billion in property damage. The US government sent in members of the US Marines, US Army, and National Guard to quell the violence.

In the wake of the unrest, the city instituted some reforms, such as limiting the terms of police chiefs—who, at the time of King's beating, could serve indefinitely. However, many observers thought the reforms were insufficient, and the LAPD continued to face accusations of excessive force in later years.

In 1992 a jury acquitted four white police officers of wrongdoing in the severe beating of black Los Angeles resident Rodney King. The verdict outraged many black Angelenos, some of whom rioted in protest. National media heavily covered cases of looting, vandalism, and other violence on the city's streets.

Many US industries rely heavily on the labor of migrant workers from Latin America, who often face poor working conditions and prejudice in the United States. In this photo, agricultural workers harvest iceberg lettuce in California.

As a result of this cheap labor, industries earned huge profits and American consumers became accustomed to paying low prices for the products and services the workers supported. Meanwhile, many white American workers feared that employers' preference for the cheap labor of immigrants would hurt their own job prospects. The perception that all people of Latin American descent are in the country illegally—and are guilty of drug-related crimes—gained traction with the American public. According to the Pew Hispanic Center, the nation's Latino population was fifty million in 2010, while the population of unauthorized immigrants that year was only one-fifth of that, at a little over eleven million people. In the early decades of the twenty-first century, crackdowns on illegal immigration at local, state, and federal levels have put Latinos at high risk for racial profiling, including heightened scrutiny by local police departments and US Border Patrol officials.

Across the nation, Latinos are more likely than white people to be stopped by law enforcement while walking or driving—and they are often detained for hours even when it is clear they have not committed any crime. Latino Americans such as landscape architect Richard Gallego express frustration at the unequal treatment. "I'm a US citizen. If the law tells you to ask me for my immigration status, that should go for everyone—not just Latinos. But these laws are only for Latinos. Nobody's talking about Turkish, Japanese, Indian, or Canadian illegal immigrants." Gallego's assessment is backed up by data. In 2010 Mexicans made up about 58 percent of the estimated total of unauthorized immigrants, while the remaining 42 percent came from numerous other nations.

The activities of Mexican drug cartels, which often hire or coerce undocumented immigrants to smuggle drugs into the United States, intensified law enforcement interaction with—and negative public perceptions of—Latino Americans. Many Americans, including political leaders, associate Latino people with drug use and trafficking. Republican presidential candidate Donald Trump referenced these impressions during the 2016 presidential race. In the June 2015 speech in which he announced his candidacy, he remarked, "When Mexico sends its people, they're not sending the best. . . . They're sending people that have lots of problems and they're bringing those problems [with them]. They're bringing drugs, they're bringing crime. They're rapists and some, I assume, are good people, but I speak to border guards and they're telling us what we're getting."

Profiling in the Age of Global Terrorism

Latino immigrants are not the only foreign-born Americans to face racial profiling in the twenty-first century. Widespread fear and suspicion of Muslims—also known as Islamophobia—took root in the United States in the aftermath of terrorist attacks on September 11, 2001. On that day, the militant Islamist group al-Qaeda carried out a series of carefully coordinated strikes in New York and near Washington, DC, killing more than three thousand people.

Because the 9/11 terrorists came from countries in the Middle East, the region where Islam originated, many Americans came to associate Muslims with people of Middle Eastern descent, particularly Arabs (one of many Middle Eastern Arabic-speaking groups). In fact, Islam is practiced all over the world by people of various ethnic, racial, and cultural backgrounds, and people of Middle Eastern heritage practice a variety of religions, including Christianity. Yet in the United States, Islamophobia often targets anyone who "looks" Muslim. Because many (although not all) people of Middle Eastern descent have brown skin, skin color has become a primary focus in the profiling of Muslims.

Beginning around 2010, Islamophobia intensified again as a brutal terrorist organization known as the Islamic State (also called ISIS, ISIL, Daesh, and al-Sham) arose in Iraq and began to spread throughout the Middle East, gaining recruits from all over the world. ISIS carries out vicious and lethal attacks, often on small groups of Westerners or against other individuals they view as enemies of their deeply conservative understanding of Islam. After high-profile ISIS attacks gained global attention, many young Muslim and Arab Americans reported facing heightened tension and bullying at school and elsewhere. Ferida Osman, a twenty-one-year-old student in New York, was on her way home one day in November 2015 when a passerby spit on her and she heard someone shout, "Go back home, you terrorist." Fearing such encounters—or worse—many girls felt reluctant to wear hijab, traditional modest Muslim clothing, including headscarves. Some young Arab Americans began going by Americanized versions of their names (such as Mo instead of Mohammed), stopped praying in public, and no longer spoke Arabic around non-Arab friends. Nineteen-year-old Shafiq Majdalawieh, a student at Brooklyn College in New

Profiling of Muslim Americans as potential terrorists has spiked in the first two decades of the twenty-first century. Muslim women who wear hijab, traditional clothing including headscarves, often arouse suspicion and hostility. Hidayah Martinez Jaka wore a headscarf with an American flag design to highlight her patriotism when she attended a 2015 speech by Democratic presidential candidate Martin O'Malley in Virginia.

Vandals defaced this Dearborn, Michigan, mosque (Islamic house of worship) and other mosques in the area with racist graffiti in 2007. The Islamic Center of America, which houses this mosque, also received hate mail after hosting a press conference to complain about Northwest Airlines's discriminatory treatment of a group of Muslim passengers.

York, described the feeling "that everybody's out to get you and you have something to prove. . . . It feels like they're trying to shoot down our dreams and aspirations simply because we practice a different religion."

Adults also began to detect mistrust from non-Muslims. Takhia Hussein, a high school teacher in New York, says, "When my students get up to say the Pledge of Allegiance, I'm up there with them, pledging every single day. It's devastating to think people are questioning our loyalty to a country that we love."

"Why Go Back to the Past?"

In the United States of the twenty-first century, racial profiling is only the tip of the iceberg of racial inequality, deeply interwoven within a larger historical framework of exploitation and discrimination. Racial profiling as a modern phenomenon has historical origins in both individual minds and in institutional traditions. Stereotypes invented and perpetuated by white Americans for profit and power came to pervade US society, shaping attitudes and systems that still influence how people of color are treated. The importance of this legacy is clear to lawyer G. Douglas Jones, who in 2001 prosecuted two former KKK members for the 1963 bombing of Birmingham's Sixteenth Street Church. For Jones, understanding the history that shapes modern biases is a crucial step toward alleviating injustice. "People will say, 'Why go back to the past?' . . . But you never close those chapters, which still sear in the black community."

Racial profiling affects people of color in all aspects of life, including education.

CHAPTER 3
CONTEMPORARY INEQUALITY

Racial profiling in the United States is an outgrowth of institutional racism, the patterns of racial bias that are woven into every facet of American life. The racial biases that underlie institutional racism are not always overt and may even be unintentional. (These are often called implicit biases.) Nevertheless, entrenched societal racism pervades education, employment, housing, health care, politics, business, and the criminal justice system. It is often most visible in the ways in which systematic racial profiling results in fewer opportunities, more health risks, and higher poverty rates for people of color than for white Americans. People of color are substantially more likely than white people to live below the poverty line. (The poverty line is a government measure of household income below a certain level of which families qualify for government assistance programs.) For instance, the Economic Policy Institute reports that 27.4 percent of African Americans live in poverty, compared to 26.6 percent of Latino Americans and 9.9 percent of European Americans. The disparity between black Americans and European Americans is even greater among children, with 45.8 percent of black children and 14.5 percent of white children under the age of six living in poverty. This widespread economic inequality arises from—and perpetuates—a cycle of racial profiling in which institutions and individuals perceive people of color as less intelligent, underperforming, and criminally minded.

Profiling in the Classroom

As early as preschool, students in the US public school system encounter unequal treatment based on race. According to a 2014 study by the Department of Education and the Department of Justice (DOJ), black students make up only 18 percent of children enrolled in US preschools. Yet they represent 48 percent of preschoolers who received more than a single out-of-school suspension. The report also found that all students of color, regardless of grade level, face a higher likelihood of being suspended from school than do white students and that black students are suspended or expelled three times more often than white students.

Other children of color faced higher rates of discipline too. For example, American Indian children make up less than 1 percent of public school students in the United States but represent 2 percent of out-of-school suspensions and 3 percent of expulsions. The report notes that disparity is "not explained by more frequent or more serious misbehavior by students of color." Thena Robinson-Mock of the Advancement Project—a civil rights advocacy organization—emphasizes that the majority of disciplinary actions are for relatively small offenses. "There's this idea that young people are pushed out of school for violent behavior, and that's just not the case—it's things like truancy [missing school], cellphone use, not having supplies, and uniform violations." Time out of the classroom causes students to fall behind in their schoolwork. Faced with repeated punishment and a lack of support from teachers and administrators, many students of color internalize the idea that they are unlikely to succeed academically, and their performance slips to match this expectation.

Beyond the greater likelihood of institutionalized punishment, students of color face other forms of racial bias in the classroom. For instance, studies show that teachers—particularly white teachers—recommend black and Latino students for gifted programs at much lower rates than white students. Similarly, some school districts have put students of color into remedial or special education courses even though their intelligence is on par with that of their white peers. This too fits into an institutionalized profile of children of color that assumes they are intellectually inferior to white children.

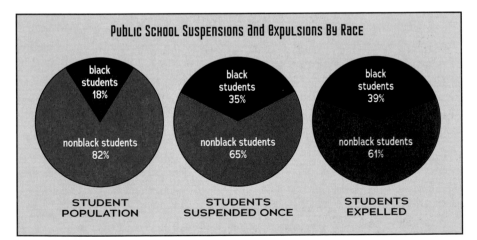

Public School Suspensions and Expulsions By Race

black students 18%
nonblack students 82%
STUDENT POPULATION

black students 35%
nonblack students 65%
STUDENTS SUSPENDED ONCE

black students 39%
nonblack students 61%
STUDENTS EXPELLED

In a 2012 nationwide study of seventy-two thousand schools in seven thousand districts, the US Department of Education found that African American students are disproportionately likely to be suspended or expelled.

According to the National Center for Education Statistics, high school graduation rates are consistently lower for students of color than for white students. The top chart at right shows data from the 2013–2014 school year. Similarly, young people of color are less likely than white people to enroll in college, as shown by the data from the 2014–2015 school year. Racial profiling by secondary school faculty and staff can contribute to lack of opportunities for students of color to succeed academically.

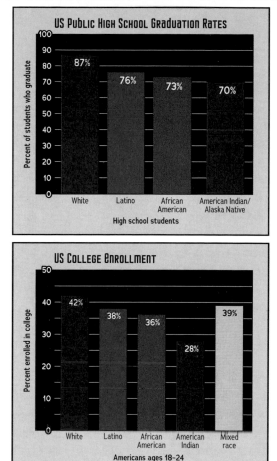

US Public High School Graduation Rates

Percent of students who graduate

- White: 87%
- Latino: 76%
- African American: 73%
- American Indian/ Alaska Native: 70%

High school students

US College Enrollment

Percent enrolled in college

- White: 42%
- Latino: 38%
- African American: 36%
- American Indian: 28%
- Mixed race: 39%

Americans ages 18–24

All these factors contribute to a lower high school graduation rate for students of color than for white students.

Such inequalities persist in higher education, where students of color often face profiling from their white peers. Blatant profiling, such as the unofficial but systematic exclusion of people of color from certain parties and student groups, has been reported at numerous campuses. Subtler race-based attitudes and judgments are even more common. Some white students may assume that students of color were admitted to college to fulfill a diversity quota rather than because of their academic qualifications. Others may hold negative stereotypes about the lifestyles of people of color.

"COOL CLOCK, AHMED"

In September 2015, fourteen-year-old Ahmed Mohamed headed to school—MacArthur High School in Irving, Texas—with a project he was eager to show off to his engineering teacher. It was an alarm clock he had made himself. But when the clock beeped during one of Ahmed's classes, school officials called police on the suspicion that the device was a bomb. The police confiscated the clock, placed Ahmed in handcuffs, and took him to a juvenile detention center where they interrogated him and took his fingerprints. Ahmed was also suspended from school for three days.

Ahmed's story soon attracted national media attention. Many observers speculated that if Ahmed had been white instead of Arab American, he might not have been treated with the same level of suspicion. Irving police chief Larry Boyd acknowledged, "We have no evidence to support that there was an intention [by Ahmed] to create alarm or cause people to be concerned." Still, Boyd defended the actions of the school and the police department, saying that authorities would have responded the same way regardless of Ahmed's race and that "you can't take things like that to school." Ahmed denied that he had acted inappropriately. "I really don't think it's fair," he said, "because I brought something to school that wasn't a threat to anyone. I didn't do anything wrong. I just showed my teachers something and I ended up being arrested."

Olevia Boykin, a black student at the University of Notre Dame in Indiana, noticed that her white fellow students "have this image of ghetto black people as portrayed in the media." Professors and other authority figures may consciously or unconsciously hold these assumptions as well, especially given that the vast majority of college and university faculty members are white. A 2015 report by the National Center for Science and Engineering Statistics (NCSES) found that people of color (excluding people of Asian descent) make up only 8 percent of the faculty at the nation's four-year colleges and universities. Black students at colleges and universities are more likely to face accusations of cheating than white students. And in general, students of color feel that others judge them based only on their race. Mariama Suwaneh, a black Latina student at the University of Washington, recalls the pressure of being the only student of color in a lecture class with hundreds of students: "I do feel like every time I raise my hand, I speak for all black people. If I say something that seems out of place, or something that doesn't sound as intelligent as another student, that's a knock on all students of color here on campus."

Racially biased attitudes and treatment can lead to feelings of isolation and stress. These are among the many factors that make students of color less likely than white students

VOICES OF EXPERIENCE

"When I was 19 years old, I was turned away from a party because I am black. . . . I was asked to show my ID. The security guards wanted to see a state ID and not my student one. When I couldn't produce it, they shooed me away with their flashlights and told me to get off the property. . . . I saw a group of white girls walk straight in without getting their IDs checked. A friend whose boyfriend worked security for the frat that night told me members of the fraternity instructed security not to grant entry to black girls for fear the Los Angeles Police Department would be more likely to break up a mixed-race party."

—Jordyn Holman, student at the University of Southern California, 2015 to graduate from two- and four-year colleges. (Other factors include financial difficulties and the failure of high schools to prepare students of color for the college experience. They also include conditions linked to poverty, low expectations, and other aspects of institutionalized racial bias.)

For students of color who graduate from four-year programs and go on to graduate school, stereotyping and

MICROAGGRESSIONS

"The limited representation of my race in your classroom does not make me the voice of all black people."

"When I gave a speech about racism, the emcee introduced me as 'Jaime Garcia.' My name is Jaime Rodriguez; not all Latinos have the last name Garcia."

"No, where are you really *from*?"

"You don't act like a normal black person ya know?"

College students shared these questions, comments, and experiences with photographer Kiyun Kim. A college student at Fordham University in New York, Kim wanted to document the subtle racial bias she saw and felt at her campus. They are all examples of racial microaggressions. As defined by Columbia University psychologist Derald Wing Sue, these are "everyday insults, indignities, and demeaning messages sent to people of color by well-intentioned white people who are unaware of the hidden messages being sent." These unspoken messages often indicate unconscious biases. Sue provides examples of these microaggressions, such as a white woman holding her purse more tightly when a black man passes, or a white person complimenting a Latino or Asian person on his or her good English, implying that the person of color is an outsider.

Microaggressions may appear to be insignificant at first. But they gather weight and meaning over time, as they occur day after day, consistently calling into question the value and the lives and experiences of people of color.

Students of color who enroll in higher education often struggle to succeed in subtly uncomfortable or overtly hostile environments. Many encounter the persistent expectation, based on their race, that they will underachieve. A lack of support from peers, faculty, and staff can help turn these expectations into a self-fulfilling prophecy. Students of color have significantly lower college graduation rates than white students—as shown by 2010 data from the Education Trust, an advocacy group for disadvantaged students.

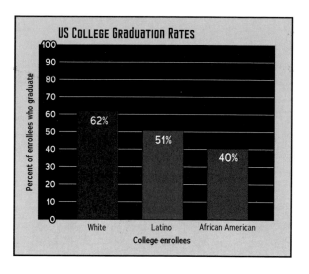

discrimination continue at the highest levels of education. A 2014 study published in the *Journal of Applied Psychology* found that college and university professors who received student inquiries about doctoral (PhD) research opportunities were most likely to respond to students whose names suggested that they were white men. Brandon, a graduate student of color studying applied physics, recalls, "I was trying to talk to [a professor] about his research and his response was, 'Well, I didn't think your kind would be interested in this kind of research.'"

Employment Obstacles

Johnny R. Williams has a degree from a prestigious university and a strong professional background. But when he found himself struggling to land interviews for jobs, he revised his résumé with a specific goal—to make it less obvious that he is black. For example, he removed a reference to his membership in an African American association. "If they're going to X me, I'd like to at least get in the door first," he explained.

Like Williams, many people of color face obstacles in employment related to racial profiling. A landmark 2003 study by the National Bureau of Economic Research found that applicants with names that suggest a black identity are called in for interviews less often than those with names that imply European American heritage. Other studies show that white applicants who have been convicted of felonies are as likely or even more likely to be called back for interviews as black applicants without criminal records. Employers also tend to view black applicants as more likely than white applicants to use drugs, as well as less likely to have the necessary work ethic and interpersonal skills to perform well.

These profiling trends suggest an institutionalized perception of workers of color as less qualified than white applicants. Profiling helps explain why—according to a study published in the *Journal of Labor Economics*—white, Latino, and Asian managers hire more white and fewer black applicants than black managers do. Daniel L. Ames, a researcher at the University of California, Los Angeles, explains that this kind of bias is often completely unconscious. "If you ask someone on the hiring committee, none of them are going to say they're racially biased. They're not lying. They're just wrong."

Intentional or not, racial bias plays out on the job as well. Many workers of color report that white coworkers tend to doubt their qualifications and expect them to underperform, reacting with obvious surprise when they excel.

Race-based assumptions can result in fewer opportunities for people of color in the workplace. Nationwide, African Americans are less likely to be promoted and more likely to be laid off than white employees. Veterinary immunologist

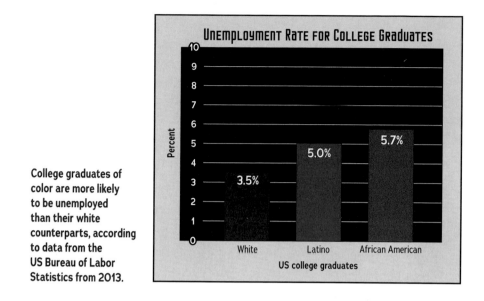

UNEMPLOYMENT RATE FOR COLLEGE GRADUATES

College graduates of color are more likely to be unemployed than their white counterparts, according to data from the US Bureau of Labor Statistics from 2013.

White: 3.5%
Latino: 5.0%
African American: 5.7%

US college graduates

Gabriela Calzada had a similar experience when she applied for a coveted job. "I had all the qualifications to get it," says Calzada. "I think they didn't give it to me because I'm Hispanic. . . . [The successful applicant] only had a bachelor's degree, and I have a Ph.D." Thirty-three percent of workers in management positions are white, while 22 percent are black and 14 percent are Latino. And 90 percent of the nation's chief executive officers—the power players in corporate America—are white.

Income Inequality

People of color face a significant wage gap: a disparity between what they earn and what white Americans earn. The typical (median) African American household earns about 40 percent less than the typical white household. Factors such as a lower level of education and other barriers to higher-paying jobs contribute to this gap, but in some industries, people of color earn less than white coworkers with equivalent jobs.

For instance, a 2014 analysis by the American Institute for Economic Research revealed that in the computer technology industry, Latino workers earned an average of $16,353 less than non-Latino workers in the same types of jobs. Black workers earn an average of $3,656 less per year than white workers, while Asian Americans earned $8,146 less than white workers. The same study found that highly skilled black finance workers earned $20,691 less per year than white workers with the same job. Highly skilled Latino workers earn $9,328 less than non-Latino workers.

This statistically lower earning power makes it much more difficult to support a family and to save money for future goals and needs. In 2013 a national study reported a $131,000 difference between the net worth of a typical white family and that of a typical black family. Studies show that about

25 percent of African American families have less than $5 of savings, compared to $3,000 for the poorest 25 percent of white families. If these families face unexpected emergencies such as serious illnesses or the loss of a job, the effects can be devastating.

Studies also show that black families are more likely than white families to be sued for their debts. The process often begins with debt collection agencies, which seek out people who owe money to credit card companies, medical providers, retailers, utility companies, and other creditors. Collection agencies and creditors themselves can sue debtors for failing to repay the money they owe. (People in dire financial situations can file for bankruptcy, but depending on the type of bankruptcy, they may remain responsible for certain debts or are vulnerable to future financial troubles that can create fresh debts. Many debtors also lack reliable resources to help them understand how to file for bankruptcy.) If a court decides in favor of a debt collector, the collector may take money out of the debtor's paycheck as part of a repayment plan or confiscate property connected to the debt (known as repossession). Debtors who violate a court order or fail to appear in court can face jail time.

All these consequences can drive people into even deeper debt. And race plays a part in how courts typically decide a debtor's case. A 2015 study by the investigative journalism organization ProPublica found that courts ruled against debtors about twice as often in mostly black communities as they did in mostly white areas. As one of the study's authors noted, "If you are black, you're far more likely to see your electricity cut, more likely to be sued over a debt, and more likely to land in jail because of a parking ticket."

RACIAL PROFILING AND VOTING RIGHTS

The Voting Rights Act of 1965 outlawed racial discrimination in voting practices by the federal, state, and local governments. Yet barriers to voting still exist for many Americans of color. As of 2016, thirty-four states have laws requiring voters to present identification before being permitted to cast a ballot. Nine of those states require a photo ID (such as a driver's license or passport), which many low-income Americans cannot afford. Supporters of these laws say they aim to prevent voter fraud—such as a noncitizen or otherwise ineligible person voting under a false identity. Critics, however, point out that these laws disproportionately prevent poor Americans of color from voting.

In particular, a 2014 report by a team of political scientists from several state universities alleges that members of the Republican Party are profiling racial and ethnic minority groups as likely Democratic Party supporters and are deliberately using voter ID laws to disenfranchise these voters. In legal cases across the country, courts have ruled that state voter ID laws discriminate

After signing the Voting Rights Act of 1965 into law, President Lyndon Johnson hands his pen to activist Martin Luther King Jr. Civil rights advocates such as King worked for years to gain legislators' support for antidiscrimination laws. Despite these laws, however, access to voting remains limited for many people of color.

against Latino and black voters. However, a 2014 Supreme Court decision dismissed the charge that voter ID laws are inherently racially discriminatory.

Redistricting practices pose another obstacle to people of color. Each state is divided into several types of electoral districts. Within a congressional district, residents elect a member of the US House of Representatives. In state legislative districts, residents elect lawmakers to the state senate and house. In each category, districts must have roughly equal populations. Every ten years, state lawmakers redraw district boundaries to account for population shifts in the state. Lawmakers also often work to shape districts in ways that benefit their party—ensuring that as many districts as possible contain a majority of their party's supporters. Redistricting frequently results in strangely shaped districts that snake across different neighborhoods, rather than reflecting an area's actual population demographics. The process, called gerrymandering, has historically disenfranchised people of color by dividing their communities into multiple districts, where their votes are counterbalanced by votes from white citizens.

While both parties engage in gerrymandering, Democrats frequently accuse Republican lawmakers of dividing up Democratic-leaning voters of color into different districts so that their votes carry less weight. For instance, Republicans redrew districts in seven states after the 2010 US census. In the 2012 state elections, 16.7 million citizens of these states voted for Republicans while 16.4 million voted for Democrats. Yet despite this extremely close popular vote, seventy-three Republican candidates were elected compared to only thirty-four Democratic candidates. Democratic votes had been spread out across different districts, where they were outnumbered by Republican votes.

While Republican lawmakers generally deny charges of deliberate racial discrimination in their district mapping, many acknowledge the strong association between people of color and Democratic votes. At a Republican Party event in Texas in 2013, an attendee asked, "What can Republicans do to get black people to vote?" Republican activist Ken Emanuelson replied, "I'm going to be real honest with you. The Republican Party doesn't want black people to vote if they are going to vote 9-to-1 for Democrats."

"White Tenants Only": Housing and Loans

Celeste Barker, an African American woman living in Ohio, was interested in a townhouse she'd seen listed for rent. But when she went to the rental office for more information, the property manager told her the home was no longer available. Barker reported the incident to a local fair housing group, which assigned a white person and a black person to call the agency about the same property. The property manager set up an appointment for the white caller to view the house the next day. He told the black caller that the house was unavailable.

Barker's experience reflects the challenges that renters and buyers of color confront when trying to find homes. A 2012 Housing and Urban Development (HUD) report found that people of color seeking to rent apartments and buy homes were told about fewer available properties than white people, sometimes even being told (falsely) that nothing was available.

The same pattern applied when people toured units, with real estate and rental agents showing fewer options to people of color. In some cities, studies have also found that landlords are more likely to conduct background checks on renters of color than prospective white tenants. One white landlord in New York City confessed to a *New York Magazine* reporter in 2015, "In every building we have, I put in white tenants. They want to know if black people are going to be living there. . . . They see black people and get all riled up, they call me: 'We're not paying that much money to have black people live in the building.' If it's white tenants only, it's clean." Discriminatory profiling against buyers and renters of color helps explain why even wealthy Americans of color tend to live in lower-income neighborhoods than white Americans.

When home buyers of color seek home loans to help cover the cost of their purchase, they encounter roadblocks that echo twentieth-century redlining practices. In 2013 black and Latino home buyers were denied loans more than twice as often as white buyers with similar financial profiles. This is one reason that home ownership in the United States is lower among people of color than among white people. In 2016, 42 percent of black households and 45 percent of Latino households owned homes, compared to 72 percent of white households. Studies also show that people of color who do secure home loans often pay higher interest rates than white borrowers—even white borrowers with similar economic footing and credit history. Partly as a result of these discriminatory practices, black people are more than five times as likely as white people to live in neighborhoods with high rates of poverty—areas that also typically have less access to high-quality schools and other resources.

In general, people of color face greater difficulty obtaining loans than their white counterparts do or they may be given less desirable loan terms. For example, reports show that when black and Latino car buyers seek loans to buy automobiles, creditors tend to charge them higher interest rates than white borrowers. Similarly, a 2014 study focused on entrepreneurs of color who sought loans to start or improve small businesses, comparing their experiences to those of white borrowers with similar financial profiles. This study found that borrowers of color faced more questions about their finances, received less information about their options, and were less likely to be offered help in filling out applications. The study quoted an anonymous black man who spoke about the impact of these challenges: "My self-esteem and confidence are strong, and yet I'm being denied [a loan], so it makes me feel bad about myself, bad about my business. . . . You're made to feel like [you're] just not competent or capable. I feel very, very insecure."

Environmental Racism

Barriers to desirable housing are one reason that families of color are more likely than white children to live in neighborhoods with fewer resources, higher crime rates, and a higher exposure to health risks. And because communities of color tend to have less political and socioeconomic power than majority-white communities, they often have little say in what types of industry and development take root around them.

People living in poor and heavily nonwhite neighborhoods tend to be in closer proximity to toxic waste dump sites, pollution-producing power plants, and other hazardous facilities. Even within the same community, people of color are more likely than white residents to be exposed to harmful air pollution and other health risks. For instance, a 2014 study by the University of Minnesota found that people of color are exposed to 38 percent higher levels of nitrogen dioxide than white people in the same town or city. Nitrogen dioxide—a pollutant produced by automobiles, construction equipment, and industrial operations—is linked to asthma and heart disease. Many communities of color, particularly Latino communities, also lack adequate water treatment and sewer services, which puts residents at risk for certain kinds of cancer, liver disease, and other potentially deadly illnesses. Between 1996 and 2013, communities of color filed 265 complaints with the federal Environmental Protection Agency's (EPA) Office of Civil Rights, claiming that nearby polluters had engaged in environmental discrimination. The EPA has dismissed 95 percent of these claims, the majority without any investigation. This greater likelihood of hazardous conditions, combined with the lower likelihood of intervention from authorities, is sometimes called environmental racism.

A prominent case of alleged environmental racism emerged in Flint, Michigan, in 2015. Flint is among the nation's poorest cities, with 40 percent of the population living below the poverty line—and more than half the population is African American. In 2015 corroded water pipes leached dangerously high lead levels into Flint's public drinking water supplies. Lead poisoning can have severe long-term health effects, especially for children. According to the World Health Organization, "Lead affects children's brain development resulting in reduced intelligence quotient (IQ), behavioral changes such as shortening of attention span and increased antisocial behavior, and reduced educational attainment." Michigan's governor, Rick Snyder, commissioned a task force of experts to study the origins of the crisis in October 2015 and declared a state of emergency in January 2016.

RACIAL PROFILING AND HEALTH CARE

Institutionalized racism impacts physical health and well-being. Because large numbers of people of color work in low-paying jobs that do not provide benefits, these families are less likely to have health insurance. Only about half of African American workers receive coverage through their employers, for instance. As a result, people of color often struggle to afford health care or avoid seeking care because they fear they'll be unable to pay for it. Moreover, the US health-care system has a history of performing agonizing medical experiments on black Americans, forcibly sterilizing women of color, and ignoring issues of informed consent in performing dangerous or new medical treatments on people of color.

Those who do seek care often receive substandard treatment in understaffed and poorly equipped clinics. Numerous studies show that racial and ethnic minority patients routinely receive lower-quality care than white patients—and not only because of cost and access concerns. A landmark study by the Institute of Medicine found that physicians tend to perceive their African American patients as less educated, less intelligent, more likely to abuse drugs and alcohol, and less likely to stick to treatment routines than white patients. Ronald Wyatt, a black physician, dealt with "a white physician who was openly hostile to me during a procedure, threatening that if I did not 'hold still' I could be blinded by what he was doing. . . . Making matters worse was the fact that as I waited to be seen that day, I had noticed how kind and courteous he had been to the white patients who were being seen, so I had expected the same. The treatment was not equal, and if a physician and medical director [like me] cannot get equal treatment, what chance does the average minority [patient] stand?"

Studies show that people of color believe white physicians give them substandard care, another factor that causes many people of color to avoid seeking health care entirely. Whether they receive poorer care or are afraid to pursue care at all, the consequences of such racial disparities can be deadly. In fact, life expectancy among black men is five years less than that of white men, and three years lower for black women than for white women.

In March the task force issued its report, which stated that government bodies at all levels had failed to respond appropriately to early reports of water contamination. According to the task force, Flint's state-appointed managers had prioritized money-saving measures over public safety, the Michigan Department of Environmental Quality had failed to recognize the problem soon enough, and the EPA had neglected to step in despite being aware of the contamination as early as April 2015. The report concluded, "Flint residents, who are majority black or African-American and among the most impoverished of any metropolitan area in the United States, did not enjoy the same degree of protection from environmental and health hazards as that provided to

Lead-tainted drinking water sparked a health crisis in the poor, majority-black city of Flint, Michigan. Residents were forced to use bottled water after the contamination was revealed. Here, a young person brings cases of water to a Flint home.

other communities." State representative Dan Kildee went a step further. Contending that unconscious racial bias often determines which communities receive the most government funding and attention, he said, "Places like Flint [with large black populations living in poverty] get written off."

"Racism without Racists"

With less earning power and more economic vulnerabilities, people of color occupy a less powerful position in US society than white Americans. In turn, these disadvantages reinforce a false impression that people of color are underachievers who

Communities of color traditionally receive few resources and little support from government and business institutions. Residents of American Indian reservations, for instance, often have very limited access to education, jobs, health care, and other infrastructure. This Oglala Lakota boy lives on the Pine Ridge Indian Reservation in South Dakota, where about half the residents live below the poverty line.

simply lack the intelligence or the work ethic of white people. Profiling based on these misconceptions fuels a cycle of widespread inequality.

Sociology professor Eduardo Bonilla-Silva of Duke University in North Carolina describes the influence of these subtle racial biases as "racism without racists," because many white Americans are unaware that racial bias is influencing their actions or shaping the systems in which they participate. "Instead of saying as they used to say during the Jim Crow era that they do not want us as neighbors [white people] say things nowadays such as 'I am concerned about crime, property values and schools.' . . . The 'new racism' is subtle, institutionalized, and seemingly nonracial." People of color feel the consequences of these attitudes in every aspect of American life, from preschool to the professional world.

Protesters march against New York City's stop-and-frisk policy in a 2012 demonstration.

CHAPTER 4
CRIMINAL JUSTICE AND INJUSTICE

The US Constitution has provisions to protect all Americans from injustices, mistreatment, and discrimination, including at the hands of police officers and other agents of the law. The Fourteenth Amendment to the US Constitution states, in part: "No state shall make or enforce any law which shall abridge the privileges or immunities of citizens of the United States; nor shall any state deprive any person of life, liberty, or property, without due process of law; nor deny to any person within its jurisdiction the equal protection of the laws." The Fourth Amendment requires that law enforcement officials have a good reason—known legally as probable cause—for searching individuals or their property, or for making an arrest. In addition, criminal procedural rules include the Miranda warning, also called Miranda rights. This rule requires law enforcement officials to inform individuals of their rights—

including the right to an attorney and the right to remain silent during questioning as they are taken into custody.

In practice, these laws and constitutional protections are not always applied consistently. For many Americans, the likelihood that they will face arrest, mistreatment, or injury depends largely on their appearance—especially skin color. Studies by government agencies, civil rights organizations, and independent researchers show that in the United States, law enforcement profiling contributes to statistically higher numbers of police stops and arrests of people of color—often for minor infractions such as drug possession or traffic violations—than of white people. Black and Latino Americans are also more likely than white Americans to face police brutality—excessive use of force by law enforcement officers.

Legal scholars also connect racial profiling statistics to higher rates of incarceration among people of color than among white Americans. Some studies suggest that African American males carry out more violent crimes and more property crimes than people of other races. Yet the difference in the rate of crime is not significant enough to account for the disparity in arrest and incarceration rates for these crimes.

A similar disparity exists with drug-related cases. According to 2009 statistics from the National Council on Crime and Delinquency, black Americans made up 13 percent of the population and 14 percent of illegal drug users, a statistical relationship that is not out of proportion. Numerous studies since the 1980s have shown that black Americans are, in fact, no more likely to be drug users or sellers than white Americans. Yet black Americans represented 37 percent of the people arrested on drug-related charges, as well as 56 percent of those in state prisons for drug crimes. The report's author,

Jamie Fellner, attributed the disparity to the US government's war on drugs, which disproportionately targets people of color. Fellner wrote, "Jim Crow may be dead, but the drug war has never been color-blind. Although whites and blacks use and sell drugs, the heavy hand of the law is more likely to fall on black shoulders." Similar double standards apply to each aspect of the criminal justice system.

The School-to-Prison Pipeline

People of color are more likely than white Americans to encounter racial bias from law enforcement very early in life. Children of color are more likely than white children to be suspended or expelled from school and to live in poor neighborhoods with high police presence. This means they are therefore more likely to have contact with police officers in their neighborhoods. "They're out getting into trouble in places they shouldn't be at times they shouldn't be," explains Emily Morgan, a senior policy analyst for the Council of State Governments Justice Center, a nonprofit agency that focuses on public safety. "They are more likely to be picked up by law enforcement and be processed by the system."

Students of color often encounter law enforcement in their schools. At public schools that face high levels of violence and crime, school districts often hire police officers—sometimes called resource officers—to work on-site and offer an added measure of security. However, this also means that student misbehavior, which would once have been handled by teachers, principals, and other school officials, is instead turned over to law enforcement and treated as a criminal matter. In turn, behavior that might once have led to detention, suspension, or expulsion can result instead in jail time and a criminal record.

"Kids from suburban white America—they don't get arrested for cursing out a teacher, throwing a book," says Jim St. Germain of the nonprofit mentoring group Preparing Leaders of Tomorrow. "These are the things they go to a counselor for." Sometimes called the school-to-prison pipeline, this chain of events can quickly funnel students of color from school directly into the criminal justice system.

Greater police presence in schools can also lead to the more frequent use of force against students who are being disciplined. And in some of the most prominent cases, observers have pointed to race as a key factor. In November 2013, Noe Nino de Rivera, a seventeen-year-old Latino high school student in Texas, got involved in a fight between two students. A white school resource officer, Deputy Randy McMillan, used a Taser on Rivera, who fell to the floor and hit his head. While Rivera was unconscious, McMillan placed him in handcuffs. Rivera was in a coma for fifty-two days as a result of a brain injury caused by the fall. Some individuals and groups criticized the officer's actions as unnecessarily forceful. The ACLU condemned the use of Tasers on juveniles, stating, "Texas families deserve to send their children to school without fear, knowing they can trust their schools to be safe havens." The local police department, on the other hand, defended the officer's actions, saying that "Deputy McMillan used the reasonable amount of necessary force to maintain and control discipline at the school."

Another incident gained widespread attention in October 2015. At Spring Valley High School in Columbia, South Carolina, a sheriff's deputy, Ben Fields, had a confrontation with a sixteen-year-old female black student. Two cell phone videos, taken by other students in the class, showed Fields telling the girl to get up and leave the classroom. When she refused to do so, Fields flipped over the desk in which the girl was sitting, throwing her to the floor. He then dragged her from the desk and handcuffed her. When the video went viral, many viewers criticized the officer, saying that his use of force was excessive. The county sheriff fired Fields, and the FBI and the US attorney's office both launched investigations of the incident.

The officer's actions hinted at a particularly intolerant attitude toward students of color—and statistics tell a similar story. In a 2014 report, the US Department of Education found that black students made up just 16 percent of enrollment in the schools studied but represented a disproportionate 31 percent of those arrested at school, during off-campus school activities, or based on a school official's referral. By contrast, 51 percent of enrolled students were white, and they represented 41 percent of those referred to law enforcement and 39 percent of students arrested— statistics that are much more in line with the overall representation of white students in school.

The Office of Juvenile Justice and Delinquency Prevention (part of the US Department of Justice) reported in 2011 that for every 100,000 black juveniles in the nation, 521 were in a correctional facility. (Correctional facilities can include a wide range of settings from privately operated rehabilitation centers to public facilities that closely resemble adult prisons.) By contrast, 202 out of every 100,000 Latino juveniles and 112 out of 100,000 white juveniles were in correctional facilities.

Stop and Frisk

Police departments in numerous large US cities encourage police officers to stop, interrogate, and search pedestrians whom they suspect of criminal behavior. The practice, widely known as stop and frisk, first emerged as official police policy in the 1930s, when LAPD officers began stopping numerous people in areas where crimes had been reported. By the 1950s, this strategy had spread to other urban areas. In 1964 New York State passed the first stop-and-frisk law, allowing NYPD officers to stop, question, and search pedestrians for weapons or drugs. The US Supreme Court declared the practice legal in a 1968 case, *Terry v. Ohio* (giving rise to another common name for the practice: a Terry stop). In its ruling, the court determined that police officers have the legal right to stop and search an individual, without probable cause for an arrest, as long as the officers have some reasonable suspicion as a basis for the stop. By the early twenty-first century, the NYPD in particular began to draw public criticism for this policy.

Controversial stop-and-frisk policies throughout the nation involve a two-step process. First, a police officer can stop and interrogate a pedestrian. Then, if the officer believes the pedestrian may possess illegal materials, the officer can search the person for drugs or weapons.

According to a 2013 report by the New York State Office of the Attorney General, NYPD officers made 4.4 million stops between January 2004 and June 2012. And 83 percent of those stops involved black and Latino people, who each made up only 26 percent (a combined 52 percent) of New York City's total population according to the 2010 census. During those years, only about 10 percent of stop-and-frisk incidents involved white people, who comprised about 33 percent of New York City's population in 2010. This disproportionate representation of people of color in interactions with law enforcement reflects the institutionalized notion that people of color are more likely to exhibit criminal behavior.

However, no research has proven that stop and frisk reduces or prevents crime. In fact, between 2004 and 2012, police officers found guns in less than 0.2 percent of searches. Searches revealed other contraband, such as knives and illegal drugs, in 1.5 percent of stops. Only 1.5 percent of stop-and-frisk arrests led to jail time or to a prison sentence, and just 0.1 percent resulted in convictions for a violent crime or for possession of a weapon. And data showed that black and Latino suspects were actually less likely than white people to be found carrying illegal goods or substances. Yet police officers were more likely to stop a person of color and to engage in physical force during a stop.

In 2008 a civil rights legal group called the Center for Constitutional Rights sued the City of New York on the grounds that stop-and-frisk practices were unconstitutional. In 2013 federal judge Shira A. Scheindlin ruled that the way the NYPD had carried out the stop-and-frisk policy did indeed violate the Constitution's protections against racial discrimination and unreasonable searches. In her decision,

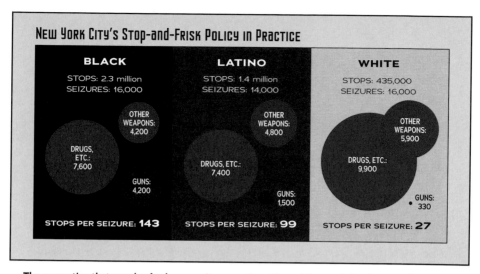

NEW YORK CITY'S STOP-AND-FRISK POLICY IN PRACTICE

BLACK

STOPS: 2.3 million
SEIZURES: 16,000

OTHER WEAPONS: 4,200

DRUGS, ETC.: 7,600

GUNS: 4,200

STOPS PER SEIZURE: **143**

LATINO

STOPS: 1.4 million
SEIZURES: 14,000

OTHER WEAPONS: 4,800

DRUGS, ETC.: 7,400

GUNS: 1,500

STOPS PER SEIZURE: **99**

WHITE

STOPS: 435,000
SEIZURES: 16,000

OTHER WEAPONS: 5,900

DRUGS, ETC.: 9,900

GUNS: 330

STOPS PER SEIZURE: **27**

The perception that people of color commit more crimes than white people has been used to justify racial profiling in stop-and-frisk practices by police officers across the country. Yet according to data gathered by the Center for Constitutional Law, white people who were stopped and searched in New York City were far more likely to possess drugs or weapons than people of color who were stopped. The chart above shows NYPD stops and seizures of illicit goods between 2004 and 2012.

she wrote that officers had demonstrated a habit of stopping "blacks and Hispanics who would not have been stopped if they were white." She also pointed out that officers were allowed to use vague and subjective reasons for conducting a stop. In particular, police could cite "furtive [sneaky] movements" as the reason for stopping someone. Scheindlin wrote, "No one should live in fear of being stopped whenever he leaves his home to go about the activities of daily life." While the judge did not order the city to end stop and frisk, she did call for changes to the policy, such as requiring officers to state more concrete reasons for making stops and creating a process for the NYPD to investigate individual complaints of racial profiling.

Even before the high-profile ruling, the NYPD's use of stop and frisk had begun to decline, and this trend continued with the support of Mayor Bill de Blasio, who took office in 2014. By 2015 police made 22,939 stops—compared to 685,724 at the policy's peak in 2011. However, even with this drop-off and with the NYPD's reforms, the practice continued to draw accusations of unreasonably targeting New Yorkers of color. The New York Civil Liberties Union (NYCLU) found that in the first half of 2015, police found no evidence of criminal activity in 80 percent of stop-and-frisk cases. Of the people stopped, 54 percent were black, 29 percent were Latino, and 11 percent were white. In certain neighborhoods, the racial disparity in the stops was even starker. For instance, as of 2011, only 24 percent of residents in Brooklyn's Park Slope neighborhood were black or Latino. Yet in that year, 79 percent of the people stopped in that neighborhood were black or Latino.

As stop and frisk declines in New York City, similar policies in other cities around the nation continue to draw criticism. In Chicago, Illinois, for instance, black people make up 32 percent of the city's population but account for 72 percent of police stops—many of which occur without clear justification. Between May and August of 2014 alone, officers conducted 250,000 stops that did not result in arrest. In a 2015 analysis of police stops in Chicago, the ACLU of Illinois found that "in nearly half of the stops we reviewed, officers either gave an unlawful reason for the stop or failed to provide enough information to justify the stop." Also in 2015, six black residents of Chicago sued the Chicago Police Department (CPD), claiming that police stops violated their constitutional rights. Later that year, under pressure from the ACLU of Illinois, the CPD agreed to implement several reforms to its stop-and-frisk policy, including more detailed record keeping that will make it possible to track where stops occur, the reasons given for the stops, which officers make the stops, and the race and ethnicity of those who are stopped. Supporters of the reforms say this information will allow more accurate analysis of the reasons stops are made, making it easier to pinpoint areas where racial profiling is a problem and even identify specific officers who rely on racial profiling. By February 2016, stop-and-frisk incidents in Chicago had decreased by 80 percent.

Traffic Stops

On July 10, 2015, Texas state trooper Brian Encinia pulled over twenty-eight-year-old Sandra Bland in Prairie View, Texas. Encinia, who identifies as Hispanic, told Bland, a black woman, that he had pulled her over for failing to signal a lane change. Dash-cam video in the trooper's car and a bystander's phone recording of the incident recorded much of the encounter that followed. When Encinia told Bland to put out her cigarette, she refused. He then ordered her to get out of the car, and she again refused. Encinia reached into the car window to grab Bland, threatening to use his Taser. He told her she was under arrest, although he did not respond when she asked "What for?" When Bland did eventually get out of the car, Encinia placed her in handcuffs and said, "You're going to jail for resisting arrest."

Legal experts who studied the footage said that while Encinia had the right to order Bland out of the car and that she should have complied with that demand, he escalated the situation without apparent cause. In jail, Bland left a voice mail for a friend expressing her disbelief that a simple traffic stop had led to her arrest. "I'm still just at a loss for words, honestly, about this whole process. How did switching lanes with no signal turn into all of this? I don't even know."

A 2011 DOJ study found that of police pulled over 15 percent of American Indian drivers, 12.8 percent of black drivers, and 10.4 percent of Latino drivers. Only 9.8 percent of white drivers were pulled over. And drivers of color were much more likely to be searched after being stopped.

Defenders of police department practices often insist that higher rates of stops for drivers of color do not necessarily indicate racial profiling. Rather, they say, people of color simply tend to make up the majority of the population in high-crime neighborhoods with a heavy police presence. In northern Dearborn Heights, Michigan, city council member Dave Abdallah used this line of reasoning when he addressed citizens' complaints of racial profiling by police. Because the area has a large Arab American population, he said, the majority of people arrested or ticketed will inevitably be Arab. "They aren't necessarily targeting anyone," Abdallah told reporters in 2016, "but they will get more Arab Americans because they happen to be there." Another rationale holds that because people of color are statistically more likely to live in poverty, they may also be more likely to drive cars with conditions (such as a broken taillight) that could lead to a stop.

Still, these factors fail to fully explain why drivers of color are disproportionately stopped and searched. An in-depth analysis by the *New York Times* in 2015 found further evidence of racial profiling in traffic stops. For example, in Greensboro, North Carolina, the study reported the following:

> Officers pulled over African-American drivers for traffic violations at a rate far out of proportion with their share of the local driving population. They

used their discretion to search black drivers or their cars more than twice as often as white motorists—even though they found drugs and weapons significantly more often when the driver was white. Officers were more likely to stop black drivers for no discernible reason. And they were more likely to use force if the driver was black, even when they did not encounter physical resistance.

For Latino drivers, traffic stops by law enforcement often go hand in hand with questions about immigration status. Near the US-Mexican border, US Border Patrol officers can legally detain and interrogate anyone they suspect of being an undocumented immigrant.

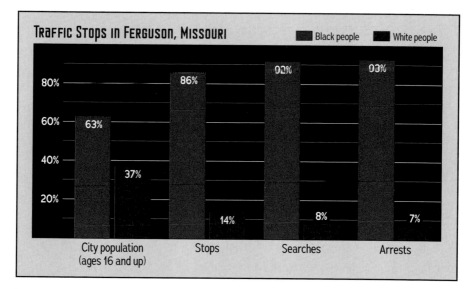

TRAFFIC STOPS IN FERGUSON, MISSOURI

Black people ■ White people

80%	86%	92%	93%
60% — 63%			
40%	37%		
20%			
	14%	8%	7%
City population (ages 16 and up)	Stops	Searches	Arrests

Throughout the United States, police officers tend to stop drivers of color disproportionately. For instance, in the city of Ferguson, Missouri, in 2013, black people made up 63 percent of the population but account for more than 80 percent of traffic stops, vehicle searches, and resulting arrests. This does not mean that black residents are committing more traffic violations than white people, but rather that police are more likely to monitor and engage with them.

In many southwestern states, state and local law enforcement also demand proof that Latino travelers are legal residents of the United States. In April 2010, Arizona enacted one of the nation's strictest and most far-reaching immigration laws yet: the Support Our Law Enforcement and Safe Neighborhoods Act, often referred to as SB 1070. Its goal is to identify, prosecute, and ultimately deport undocumented immigrants in the state. It authorizes law enforcement officials to stop and question any person, as long as they feel there is "reasonable suspicion" that the person is an undocumented immigrant. The law also requires noncitizens in the state to carry immigration documents and identification at all times. If they are stopped by law enforcement and found to be without these papers, they may face arrest. In addition, SB 1070 prohibits anyone without proper immigration documentation from applying for work in Arizona. Following the passage of SB 1070, Alabama, Georgia, Indiana, South Carolina, and Utah passed similar bills.

Supporters of SB 1070 called it an important step toward reducing illegal immigration. However, critics argued that the measure both encouraged and legalized racial profiling of Mexican Americans, other Latinos, American Indians, and others whom law enforcement might mistake for immigrants. Furthermore, critics pointed out that the law's broad allowance for reasonable suspicion effectively gives police officers the right to use skin color—as opposed to any suspicious behavior—as the reason for a stop. Given these concerns, opponents of the law said that even if it were effective in reducing illegal immigration, the civil rights costs were too high. The critics included President Barack Obama, who stated that the law could "undermine basic notions of fairness that we

Arizona's immigration law SB 1070 sparked protests against its endorsement of racial profiling, as well as against deportation of undocumented immigrants. Activists such as those shown here object to crackdowns on undocumented immigration, alleging that racial prejudice largely motivates deportation policies.

cherish as Americans, as well as the trust between police and our communities that is so crucial to keeping us safe." Mexico's then president Felipe Calderón was blunter in his comments, saying that the law "introduces a terrible idea: using racial profiling as a basis for law enforcement." Protests against the law soon took place outside the Arizona State Capitol and elsewhere. Demonstrators carried signs bearing messages such as, "Do I look 'illegal'?" and "Brown skin is not a crime." In 2012 the US Supreme Court struck down some aspects of the law but upheld others, including the requirement that police officers check the immigration status of anyone they suspect to be an undocumented immigrant.

Profiling and Police Brutality

On August 5, 2014, John Crawford III, a twenty-two-year-old black man, was shopping at a Walmart in Beavercreek, Ohio. He had picked up an air rifle (also known as a pellet gun) from a display and was carrying it around the store when a fellow shopper called 911 to report that a man in the store had a gun. Police officers arrived on the scene and fatally shot Crawford, later saying that he had ignored orders to drop the gun. However, surveillance video from the store cast doubt on the officers' report. The officers fired so soon after approaching Crawford that many viewers questioned whether there could have been time for them to issue a clear warning. Yet in September 2014, a grand jury chose not to press charges against the officers involved, stating that their actions had been justified.

Crawford's death is one of several cases that has brought increased public attention to police brutality against people of color and fueled demands for change. Among the other highly publicized incidents were the killings of eighteen-year-old Michael Brown of Ferguson, Missouri, in August 2014; fifty-year-old Walter Scott of North Charleston, South Carolina, in April 2015; twenty-five-year-old Freddie Gray of Baltimore, Maryland, also in

GROUPS MOST LIKELY TO BE KILLED by Law ENFORCEMENT

African Americans age 20–24	7.1
American Indians age 25–34	
American Indians age 35–44	
African Americans age 25–34	5.6
American Indians age 20–24	
Latinos age 20–24	4.4
Latinos age 25–34	3.2
African Americans age 35–44	3.0
African Americans age 15–19	2.9
Average, for all races and ages	1.2

Rate of law enforcement killings, per million population per year, 1999–2011

According to the Centers for Disease Control and Prevention, African Americans and American Indians are most at risk for fatal encounters with law enforcement. Their rates of death at the hands of police officers far surpass the national average of 1.2 people for every 1 million people in the United States.

Activists affiliated with the Black Lives Matter movement rally around the stories of Michael Brown *(left)*, Eric Garner *(center)*, Tamir Rice *(right)*, and other unarmed black people killed by police.

April 2015; forty-three-year-old Eric Garner of Staten Island, New York, in July 2015; thirty-seven-year-old Alton Sterling of Baton Rouge, Louisiana, in July 2016; and thirty-two-year-old Philando Castile of Saint Paul, Minnesota, in July 2016.

Throughout the United States, numerous people of color—many of whom are unarmed—die at the hands of police officers, who often do not face legal consequences. A report by the *Washington Post* found that between January 1, 2015, and July 10, 2016, 24 percent of the people fatally shot by police officers were African Americans. Because African Americans make up just 13 percent of the total US population, this data indicates they are 2.5 times more likely than white people to die by police shooting. Furthermore, the report found that police fatally shot 50 unarmed white people and 50 unarmed black people during this period. Yet the white population is about five times larger than the black population, meaning that unarmed black Americans are actually five times as likely as unarmed white Americans to be fatally shot by police.

CASE STUDY: MICHAEL BROWN

On the afternoon of August 9, 2014, Michael Brown and a friend, Dorian Johnson, were walking down the street in Ferguson, Missouri, a suburb of Saint Louis. Brown and Johnson, both black, were eighteen and twenty-two years old, respectively. They had just left Ferguson Market and Liquor, where security video later showed that an African American male had shoplifted cigarillos and shoved the store's clerk on his way out. Darren Wilson, a white officer with the Saint Louis Police Department, drove by on patrol, noticed the young men, and approached them. Based on the young men's appearance and the fact that Brown held cigarillos, Wilson may have identified Brown and Johnson as suspects in the convenience store theft.

What happened over the next few minutes is unclear, but the interaction ended with Wilson shooting Brown at least six times in the head, chest, and arm. A few minutes later, an ambulance happened to pass by the scene and a paramedic declared Brown dead. His body then lay in the street for more than four hours. A crowd, largely neighborhood residents, soon gathered. Saint Louis officials later said this disorder may have delayed authorities in collecting Brown's body. Whatever the reason for the delay, the stark sight of a dead black teenager lying in the summer sun left a deep impression. As one local put it, "You'll never make anyone black believe that a white kid would have laid in the street for four hours."

Conflicting stories about how Brown was killed soon flooded the news. Brown's friend Dorian Johnson said Brown had raised his hands and said, "Don't shoot" before Wilson fired. Other

In most of these cases, officers deny that racial profiling played a role in their decisions. However, witness testimony and video footage of incidents often indicate that racially biased targeting took place. Even so, the majority of officers implicated in using excessive force against people of color face no criminal charges. While police departments have fired officers involved in high-profile cases, disciplinary action for less publicized incidents is often much lighter.

The degree to which racial profiling plays a role in cases of police brutality is impossible to measure precisely. Taken witnesses disagreed. Some observers dwelled on the possibility that Brown may have been guilty of theft from the convenience store, while others countered that even if he had been, that crime should not have cost him his life. In November 2015, a jury chose not to indict Wilson for Brown's killing, saying that Wilson had acted in self-defense according to the law.

Did Darren Wilson treat Michael Brown differently because he was black? Some analysts have pointed out that the language in Wilson's own account of the shooting seemed to show an attitude that villainized and dehumanized Brown, including describing him as looking like "a demon." Wilson later told an interviewer, "Do I think about who [Brown] was as a person? Not really, because it doesn't matter at this point. Do I think he had the best upbringing? No. Not at all." Additionally, Wilson's actions appeared to fit into a long-standing pattern of white police officers in Ferguson targeting black residents.

This pattern was confirmed by a DOJ investigation into events in Ferguson, before and after Brown's death. The DOJ report, published in March 2015, detailed systematic bias in the Ferguson Police Department, saying that "African Americans experience disparate impact in nearly every aspect of Ferguson's law enforcement system." For instance, African Americans represented 67 percent of Ferguson's population but accounted for 85 percent of the Ferguson Police Department's traffic stops and 93 percent of its arrests between 2012 and 2014. In response to these findings, the DOJ declared that the City of Ferguson had violated citizens' constitutional rights and called on the city to carry out significant reforms to its criminal justice system. In February 2016, after the city refused the DOJ's proposed plan for reforms, the DOJ filed a civil rights lawsuit against the City of Ferguson.

together, however, fatal encounters between police officers and people of color illustrate the high costs of race-based suspicions and assumptions. Writer Bijan Stephen speaks of the toll these tragedies take on minority communities: "I, along with every other black person in America, live with fear every day."

Jailhouse Deaths

On the morning of July 13, 2015, three days after Texas state trooper Brian Encinia arrested Sandra Bland for a minor traffic violation, she was found dead, hanging in her jail cell.

Certain that she wouldn't have killed herself, her family voiced suspicions that Bland might have been harmed by police while in jail. Some of the jail's records show that Bland reported no problems with depression, while others say she had told staff at the jail that she had attempted suicide in the past. Experts say she should have been placed under close observation to make sure she did not harm herself. Jail staff did not take this precautionary step.

Bland's autopsy reported that her injuries were consistent with suicide. Nevertheless, Texas authorities began an investigation into her death, examining whether the jail employees had taken appropriate steps to ensure her safety. In December 2015, a grand jury announced that it would not indict anyone from the jail in connection with Bland's death. In January 2016, a second grand jury indicted Encinia on perjury, charging that he had not been truthful in his account of Bland's arrest.

While questions remain about what exactly happened to Bland, her story is part of a larger pattern. In the same month she died, at least four other black women—eighteen-year-old Kindra Chapman, fifty-year-old Joyce Curnell, thirty-seven-year-old Ralkina Jones, and forty-two-year-old Raynette Turner—also died in jail cells under uncertain circumstances. When people of color die in police custody, particularly in jail cells while awaiting trial or release, their deaths can often be linked to neglect on the part of jail staff. Inattention to medical conditions, from mental health issues to an inmate's need for specific medication, routinely put inmates at undue risk.

Moreover, families often find law enforcement agencies to be slow to investigate or clarify the circumstances of these deaths. For example, the day after Bland's death, fifty-three-

Twenty-eight-year-old Sandra Bland died in her Texas jail cell after being arrested during a routine traffic stop in 2015. The circumstances of her arrest and death sparked nationwide calls for police accountability.

year-old Choctaw activist Rexdale W. Henry was found dead in a Mississippi jail cell after being arrested for failing to pay a minor traffic ticket. More than two weeks later, Henry's cellmate was charged with his murder, a development that raised further questions about law enforcement's handling of the case. "I don't understand why it took so long from the time that they found Mr. Henry dead in his cell to the time they charged a cellmate for his murder," said Syracuse University law professor Janis McDonald, who assisted Henry's family with an independent investigation. "They were locked up together, why would it take 16 days?" The charge that families and advocates make is not so much that law enforcement deliberately caused an inmate's death because of racial prejudice but rather that the inmate was given less attentive care because of race—and that after this inattention resulted

CASE STUDY: FREDDIE GRAY

On the morning of April 12, 2015, a police officer in Baltimore, Maryland, made eye contact with Freddie Gray, a twenty-five-year-old black man. Gray began running, and the officer followed, calling for backup. Eventually three officers overtook Gray, handcuffed him, and searched him. Finding a knife he was carrying, they placed him under arrest.

Witnesses later said that Gray, who had asthma, asked for an inhaler, but police did not give him one. A bystander's cell phone video showed officers pulling a handcuffed Gray toward a police van as he screamed and dragged one of his legs.

The van made multiple stops on its way to a police station. Reports say that officers never buckled Gray's seat belt—a violation of Baltimore Police Department policy. By the time the van arrived at the police station, about forty-five minutes after Gray and the police officer saw each other on the corner, Gray "could not talk and he could not breath [sic]," according to city officials. He was taken to a hospital, where he died of a severe spinal cord injury on April 19.

The medical examiner who prepared Gray's autopsy report speculated that Gray might have stood up in the back of the van and then been thrown against the van's side when it abruptly slowed down or turned. The report ruled his death a homicide, saying that officers had failed to take steps, such as buckling Gray's seat belt, that could have prevented his injuries. Six officers involved in Gray's death faced criminal charges ranging from misconduct to

in the inmate's death, departments dismissed the institutional failures that created the tragic situation.

Stand Your Ground Laws

Racial bias can also impact the ways in which the criminal justice system treats people of color when they are victims of crimes. For example, people of color are often victims of beatings, killings, and other acts of violence at the hands of law enforcement officers. Few of the officers in high-profile brutality cases have received criminal convictions for their actions. Some observers argue that these cases highlight the justice system's second-degree murder. As of June 2016, one officer's trial had ended in a mistrial and two others' had resulted in acquittals.

Of the six officers charged, three were white and three were black. But some people argue that racial profiling still played a role in Gray's arrest and death. When the *Baltimore Sun* newspaper analyzed data from 2014, it found that black people make up 64 percent of Baltimore's population but represented 93 percent of arrests for loitering and 84 percent of arrests for trespassing. The *Baltimore Sun* concluded that black citizens in Baltimore are stopped and arrested disproportionately—not because they commit more crimes than white citizens but because they receive heavier police scrutiny. The paper's editorial board wrote, "It's not necessarily that the officers chased Freddie Gray because he was black, it's that he almost certainly wouldn't have been on that corner if he hadn't been." Similarly, a friend of Gray's, Rudolph Jackson, described how he and many other Baltimore residents viewed the situation: "I'm not saying Fred was an angel. . . . But the police already have made up their minds about who we are."

Near the spot where Baltimore police officers arrested Freddie Gray in 2015, a mural depicts Gray in front of the ghosts of civil rights activists and other victims of police brutality. Gray died after suffering injuries in police custody.

bias in favor of police officers rather than a racial bias.

But what about crimes committed by civilians against people of color? Such cases can reveal the ways in which the US justice system tolerates racial profiling by private citizens—and allows implicit racial bias to influence how laws are enforced. On the rainy evening of February 26, 2012, seventeen-year-old Trayvon Martin was on his way home in Sanford, Florida. Martin, who was black, was wearing a hoodie sweatshirt with the hood up as he walked through the gated subdivision where he lived. George Zimmerman, a twenty-eight-year-old man of white and Latino ethnicity, also lived in the subdivision. He led the neighborhood watch group and had been worried about recent burglaries in the area. At about seven o'clock that night, Zimmerman was driving his SUV through the neighborhood when his path crossed Martin's. Zimmerman called the police, saying that Martin seemed suspicious and might be on drugs. The dispatcher told Zimmerman that officers would check out the situation and that Zimmerman did not need to follow Martin.

Less than ten minutes later, Zimmerman fatally shot Martin in the chest.

HATE CRIMES

On February 10, 2015, in Chapel Hill, North Carolina, Craig Stephen Hicks—a white man—shot and killed twenty-three-year-old Deah Shaddy Barakat; Deah's wife, twenty-one-year-old Yusor Mohammad Abu-Salha; and Yusor's nineteen-year-old sister, Razan Mohammad Abu-Salha. All three victims were Muslims. Deah and Yusor were Hicks's neighbors and had had several confrontations with him about parking spaces and other minor issues. Following the killings, many observers felt that Hicks had targeted his victims mainly because they were Muslim.

If so, the murders would legally qualify as hate crimes. A hate crime is any crime specifically motivated by prejudice. (This can include prejudice based on gender and sexual orientation as well as race, ethnicity, religion, and national origin. People of color often fit into one or more vulnerable categories.) Hate crimes can take many forms, from defacement of places of worship to physical assault or murder.

According to the FBI, hate crimes against Muslims or Arabs—or those perceived to be either—increased after 9/11, and as of 2015, they were still five times as common as they had been before the 2001 attacks. In the wake of 2015 terrorist attacks in Europe and the United States, Muslim Americans reported more frequent experiences of being physically and verbally assaulted. Multiple mosques were vandalized around the nation, with several cases prompting FBI hate crime investigations. On social media, threats against Muslims and Arab Americans became more frequent.

Hate crimes are difficult to track. Five states lack laws against hate crimes, and across the country, police departments often fail to report hate crime statistics for their

Exactly what happened between the time Zimmerman called the police and the moment he shot Martin remains unclear. Zimmerman said that Martin attacked him and that, fearing for his life, he shot Martin in self-defense. Zimmerman was later treated for injuries to his face and head, which could have been caused by a fight with Martin. Some witnesses supported his story that Martin confronted him and perhaps began a physical altercation. But others said that Martin seemed nervous about Zimmerman following him, tried to

jurisdictions. And not all prejudice-fueled acts of violence are officially designated as hate crimes. The decision rests with local law enforcement and can be inconsistent. In June 2015, for instance, a white man fatally shot nine black parishioners at a predominantly African American church in Charleston, South Carolina. The city's police chief deemed the shooting a hate crime. On the other hand, the March 2016 murder of a Puerto Rican man and a Hmong couple in Milwaukee, Wisconsin—an incident that appears to have begun with a racist comment from the shooter—was not officially designated as a hate crime.

Residents of Washington, DC, hold a vigil in memory of three Muslim Americans murdered in a possible hate crime. A memorial poster shows a photo of Deah Shaddy Barakat *(left)*, Yusor Mohammad Abu-Salha *(center)*, and Razan Mohammad Abu-Salha *(right)*.

Even when attacks against people of color cannot be conclusively established as hate crimes, racial profiling may be at least one of the factors underlying such violence. Many hate crimes committed by civilians begin with profiling (which often misidentifies the race or ethnicity of a target) and escalate to violence. For example, many psychologists and scholars of race relations believe the killing of Trayvon Martin and the murder of Jordan Davis were racially motivated, even though they were not officially designated as hate crimes.

run away, and was overpowered by Zimmerman. A 911 call made by a neighborhood resident recorded a male voice in the background yelling for help. Martin's parents say it was their son's voice. Zimmerman's father says it was his son's voice.

George Zimmerman was a civilian, not an officer of the law, and his case highlighted another element of racial bias in the US criminal justice system. Florida's controversial self-defense law, often called the Stand Your Ground law, allows citizens to react violently to a person who they feel threatens their personal safety. Police can arrest a person who commits an act of violence only if the officers can prove that the person did not act in self-defense. Because of this law, police could take Zimmerman into custody but had to release him the same night. Zimmerman had admitted to killing Martin but claimed it was in self-defense. He was ultimately rearrested and charged with second-degree murder in April 2012.

As news of the killing spread beyond local Florida news, outrage flared across the country. Much of the conversation focused on the law and how long it took for Zimmerman to be charged. Some observers speculated that if Martin had been white, law enforcement might have acted more quickly. Meanwhile, Martin's parents began an online petition calling for Zimmerman to face trial. Martin's family lawyer described the petition as "not in an effort to persecute George Zimmerman, but in an effort to say a black 17-year-old child should be able to walk home from the store and not be shot." More than two million people signed the petition. In Sanford and Miami, Florida, demonstrators—often wearing hoodies—held protest marches calling for Zimmerman's prosecution.

In July 2013, a jury consisting of five white women and one woman of color found Zimmerman not guilty due to conflicting testimony and a lack of clear evidence that he had acted with ill intent. Civil rights advocates such as the NAACP urged the US Justice Department to file civil rights charges against Zimmerman, while also calling for an end to Stand Your Ground laws and a commitment to end racial profiling.

Less than a year after Trayvon Martin's death, the shooting death of another unarmed black teenager put the spotlight on Stand Your Ground laws once again. On November 23, 2012, four young black men—Jordan Davis, Tevin Thompson, Leland Brunson, and Tommie Stornes—pulled into the parking lot of a gas station in Jacksonville, Florida. Stornes, the car's driver, went into the gas station's convenience store, while his friends remained in the car, talking and listening to loud music. Michael David Dunn, a forty-five-year-old white man, pulled up next to them and told them to turn the music down. When seventeen-year-old Davis refused, he and Dunn started arguing through the open windows of their vehicles. Dunn then pulled a handgun from his glove compartment and began shooting just as Stornes returned. Stornes quickly drove away while Dunn continued to fire. Davis was hit twice. An ambulance rushed Davis to the hospital, where he died.

When police arrested Dunn, he told them he had felt that the young men were threatening and that he had acted in self-defense. Like George Zimmerman, he claimed a Stand Your Ground basis for his actions. Dunn added that he had seen a shotgun or maybe a stick in the car, though he also later admitted that he might have imagined it. At the 2014 trial, a jury convicted Dunn of first-degree murder and sentenced him to life in prison without parole.

Like George Zimmerman, Dunn is a civilian, not an officer of the law. And as in the killing of Trayvon Martin, not everyone believed that race was a factor in Dunn's actions or that it played a role in the outcome of the trial. Nevertheless, the incident renewed the heated public conversation about racism in the criminal justice system and about the common perception of young black males as threatening, dangerous, or likely to be guilty of criminal behavior. Davis's mother, Lucia McBath, emphasized that her son had been targeted without having done anything illegal or dangerous. "Jordan had no guns. He had no drugs. There was no alcohol. They were coming from the mall. They were being kids."

Legal scholars agree that Florida's Stand Your Ground law offered Zimmerman and Dunn a legal advantage that might not have been available to a defendant of color in a similar circumstance. A study published in the journal *Social Science & Medicine* in 2015 examined more than two hundred Florida court cases in which the Stand Your Ground law was used as a legal defense. In these cases—which spanned from 2005 to 2013—juries were twice as likely to convict perpetrators if the victims were white. "These results are similar to pre-civil rights era statistics," said the report, "with strict enforcement for crimes when the victim was white and less-rigorous enforcement when the victim is non-white."

Thirty-three states have Stand Your Ground laws. Members of the American Bar Association (a nationwide group of lawyers and law students) formed the National Task Force on Stand Your Ground Laws, which conducted a large-scale evaluation of these laws in a 2014 report. Overall, the report concluded that such laws encourage racial profiling in two ways.

CASE STUDY: WALTER SCOTT

On April 4, 2015, in North Charleston, South Carolina, Officer Michael Slager, a white man, pulled over Walter Scott, a fifty-year-old black man, for having a broken taillight on his car. Scott got out of the car and began to run away. Slager pursued him, leading to a short struggle between the men before Scott turned to run once more. Slager then fired his gun, killing Scott.

In Slager's report of the incident, he said that he had fired in self-defense, believing his life was in danger because Scott had grabbed his Taser during the scuffle. But additional information came from a bystander named Feidin Santana, who recorded the shooting on his phone. Santana's footage showed the end of the altercation and then Scott running away. As Scott fled, Slager drew his gun and fired eight times, shooting Scott in the back. The video then showed Slager walking over to Scott, who lay facedown on the ground, and cuffing Scott's hands behind his back. As a second officer arrived, Slager returned to the spot from which he'd fired and picked something up, which he then dropped next to Scott's body. Police reports said that officers gave Scott cardiopulmonary resuscitation (CPR), but this does not happen in the course of the four-minute-long video.

Scott was unarmed.

Three days after the shooting, Slager was charged with murder, and the North Charleston Police Department fired him. Even as the city reeled from the events, some observers found a measure of comfort in the fact that a murder charge was imposed so quickly, in contrast to many similar cases. Nevertheless, the details of the event—like so many before it—raised difficult questions. What if no one had recorded the incident? What if Santana had not shared the video?

A protester outside city hall in North Charleston, South Carolina, expresses his outrage over the death of Walter Scott at the hands of a police officer.

Would anyone have questioned Slager's version of events? Scott's family doesn't think so. As Scott's father put it, "It would have never come to light." City officials agreed that the video had been crucial in the decision to press charges. The North Charleston police chief said: "I have watched the video and I was sickened by what I saw." The town's mayor, Keith Summey, said he had issued an order for the city's police officers to wear body cameras, which—in the absence of a bystander like Santana—could potentially capture important information about similar events in the future.

"First . . . implicit bias may impact the perception of a deadly threat as well as the ultimate use of deadly force. Second . . . implicit bias impacts the investigation, prosecution, immunity, and final determination of which homicides are justified." The report also found that states with Stand Your Ground laws saw an increase in homicides and had no reductions in other crimes, such as theft, burglary, or assault. The report's authors recommended that states with Stand Your Ground laws repeal them—and advised other states against enacting them.

Incarceration

Stand Your Ground laws reveal only one way in which racial profiling plays out in the law enforcement and judicial systems. Experts agree that racial prejudice also contributes to mass incarceration: the high numbers of US citizens— especially people of color—behind bars. More than two million Americans are in jails or prisons across the country at any given time, and incarceration rates show a disproportionate impact on people of color.

Each year, thousands of people of color spend days, weeks, or even months in local jails while awaiting trial for minor offenses. If convicted of crimes, people of color can face years of incarceration in state or federal prisons. For every 100,000 black American males, 2,724 are in prison, while only 465 out of every 100,000 white males are imprisoned. Additionally, the Bureau of Justice Statistics has reported that American Indians are incarcerated at a rate more than 30 percent higher than the national average, despite making up less than 2 percent of the nation's population. A study by the National Council on Crime and Delinquency found that American Indian men entered prison at a rate more than four times that of white men.

Although men—regardless of racial or ethnic identity—are incarcerated at significantly higher rates than women, women of color face a greater chance of serving prison time than their white counterparts. According to the Bureau of Justice Statistics, black women are at least twice as likely to be imprisoned as white women, and Latinas are 69 percent more likely to be incarcerated than white women. The Bureau of Justice Statistics found that American Indian women are imprisoned at a rate more than six times that of white women.

Youths of color are also disproportionately represented in the criminal justice system. Statistics show that black teens are more likely than white teens to be arrested or sentenced to prison for the same crime. And the American Psychological Association found that US courts are eighteen times more likely to process, try, and sentence African American underage youth as adults (rather than as juveniles) than white youth. This trend results in harsher sentences and more serious criminal records, which in turn make it more difficult for a person to reintegrate into society after release. In all but two states, people with felony convictions are ineligible to vote while incarcerated, and many states also bar felons from voting after they serve their sentences. (Some states permanently bar felons from voting. Others allow people to formally apply for restoration of voting rights five years after the end of their sentences.) Convicted felons also can be denied public housing and are automatically disqualified for many jobs. As law professor Michelle Alexander, author of the book *The New Jim Crow*, explains, felons "are relegated to a permanent second-class status, stripped of the very rights supposedly won in the civil rights movement—like the right to vote, the right to serve on juries, the right to be free of legal discrimination and employment, and access to education and public benefits."

Sentencing

Besides being imprisoned at higher rates than white people, people of color are also, overall, imprisoned for longer than white people. In March 2010, a report by the United States Sentencing Commission found that between 2007 and 2009, black men convicted of crimes received sentences that were 23 percent longer than the white men's sentences. During that time, sentences imposed on Latino men were 6.8 percent longer than those of their white counterparts. Among American Indians, research has found that sentences are, on average, 57 percent longer than those given to white defendants.

A DOJ report also found that in federal courts, 80 percent of the defendants who were sentenced to death were racial minorities. Another study found that an African American who kills a white person is twice as likely to be sentenced to death

Treatment of people of color in jail and prison is often harsher than treatment of white inmates. For instance, studies in several states indicate that people of color are significantly more likely to be put into solitary confinement *(above)* than white people.

as a white person who kills an African American. A 2006 study for Cornell Law School also found that when jurors thought of defendants convicted of murder as having more "stereotypically black" features (designated in the study as broad noses, thick lips, dark hair, and dark skin)—and when the victims were white—juries were more than twice as likely to impose the death penalty (in states where the death penalty is an option). When the victims were also black, however, the appearance of the black defendants did not seem to affect sentencing. One of the study's researchers, criminal law expert Sheri Lynn Johnson, commented, "That disturbing result . . . is consistent with previous findings on race and the death penalty, which consistently show that black defendants accused of killing white victims are much more likely to be sentenced to death than those accused of killing blacks." Another of the study's authors, social psychologist Jennifer Eberhardt, reflected, "Race clearly matters in criminal justice in ways [of] which people may or may not be consciously aware."

CASE STUDY: ERIC GARNER

On July 17, 2014, Eric Garner was standing on a sidewalk in Staten Island, New York, when two white plainclothes police officers approached. They accused Garner, a forty-three-year-old black man, of selling loose cigarettes in violation of New York tax laws. Garner had been arrested and charged twice in the past year for selling cigarettes, as well as for marijuana possession and other low-level crimes. This time, Garner said to the arresting officers, "Every time you see me you want to arrest me. I'm tired of it. This stops today. . . . I'm minding my business, officer. Please, just leave me alone." When officers Daniel Pantaleo and Justin Damico placed him under arrest, Garner tried to brush them off, saying "Don't touch me." Pantaleo then put Garner in a choke hold, wrapping one arm tightly around his neck as additional officers arrived. Pantaleo and other officers pushed Garner to the ground, putting pressure on his chest and pressing his face against the sidewalk. As the officers placed him in handcuffs, Garner began saying, "I can't breathe." He repeated this statement eleven times while officers continued to hold him down.

After being cuffed, Garner lay on the sidewalk without moving, and officers called an ambulance. Emergency medical technicians (EMTs) arrived soon afterward but waited several more minutes before placing Garner on a stretcher. They did not administer oxygen or other life support until after he was in the ambulance. On the way to the hospital, Garner went into cardiac arrest. He was pronounced dead at 4:34 in the afternoon.

A witness's cell phone video of the arrest was picked up by news stations and posted widely on social media, generating anger and sorrow around the nation. The New York medical examiner ruled Garner's death a homicide and that the choke hold had been the cause of death. In an editorial for the digital news site the *Daily Dot*, journalist S. E. Smith argued that if Garner had been white, "police likely would not have harassed him in the first place, they would not have used such aggressive tactics to arrest him, and they would have rendered medical aid immediately, rather than standing around while he wheezed that he couldn't breathe."

Six months after Garner died, in December 2014, a grand jury decided not to press charges against Pantaleo, citing insufficient evidence of wrongdoing. Garner's mother, Gwen Carr, expressed her disbelief at the jurors' decision, asking, "Were they looking at the same video the rest of the world was looking at?"

Unconscious profiling by judges, juries, and witnesses also contributes to a higher rate of wrongful convictions of people of color than of white people. Of the 324 American inmates exonerated by genetic DNA (deoxyribonucleic acid) evidence prior to 2012, about 70 percent were people of color. Almost 75 percent of total DNA exoneration cases involve an eyewitness's misidentification of a suspect, and about 42 percent of those misidentifications are cross-racial—meaning that a witness incorrectly identified a suspect of a different race. Studies show that witnesses often struggle to distinguish facial differences among people outside their race. In other words, unconscious racial profiling can result in a conviction for an innocent person who simply happens to share the racial background of the true criminal. "Justice is color coded," says journalist David A. Love in regard to wrongful convictions, "and truly a matter of black and white."

A woman in hijab walks through the Hartsfield-Jackson Atlanta International Airport in Georgia. Muslim Americans are frequent targets of racial profiling.

CHAPTER 5
COUNTERTERRORISM AND ISLAMOPHOBIA

In August 2010, US citizen Hassan Shibly, his wife, and their baby were returning to the United States after a trip to the Middle East. Shibly said that Transportation Security Administration (TSA) officers searched his luggage and asked religiously oriented questions, including, "Are you part of any Islamic tribe? Have you ever studied Islam full time? How many gods do you believe in?"

A 2011 Pew Research survey reported that 36 percent of Muslim Americans who had flown into or out of US airports in the previous year said they had been targeted by airport security for extra screening. Airline staff and passengers also single out Muslim Americans as potential threats and take independent action. In 2016 alone, several airlines removed Muslim passengers from flights because other passengers said they felt unsafe. These incidents reflect a US government policy that takes racial profiling to a level beyond conventional law enforcement.

A Controversial Strategy

Racial profiling has been an official part of the US government's antiterrorism strategy since the creation of the Department of Homeland Security in 2002. Established in response to the September 11, 2001 terrorist attacks, this cabinet-level department has the stated goal of keeping Americans safe from a variety of threats, particularly terrorism. The DHS absorbed and reorganized a variety of existing agencies, including the TSA, US Customs and Border Protection, and US Immigration and Customs Enforcement. As part of the DHS's antiterrorism mission, workers in airport security and border patrol jobs began using race and religion as significant, authorized factors in screening to identify potential Islamist terrorists.

Some observers feel these measures are a justified use of limited profiling. However, others criticize the tactics, especially when the focus on Muslims and people of Middle Eastern descent spread beyond airport security lines and entered into questionable legal and ethical territory. For instance, following 9/11, the NYPD carried out targeted surveillance of Muslims in New York City and beyond, sending undercover officers into predominantly Muslim neighborhoods, as well as monitoring mosques and Muslim student groups. The NYPD also created files on the activities of individual Muslims. In 2012 Muslim American and civil rights groups filed a lawsuit against the City of New York, charging that the surveillance violated civil rights and was unlawfully prejudicial. The case was initially dismissed, but in 2015, a panel of three federal judges ruled that the plaintiffs had the right to pursue the lawsuit. One of these judges, Thomas L. Ambro, wrote in the panel's decision: "We have been down similar roads before. [Government

Muslim passengers on US flights frequently report being profiled by airline staff and by fellow passengers. Airline employees have asked people to get off flights if they are speaking Arabic, for instance.

policies toward] . . . African-Americans during the civil rights movement and Japanese-Americans during World War II are examples that readily spring to mind. We are left to wonder why we cannot see with foresight what we see so clearly with hindsight, that 'loyalty is a matter of the heart and mind, not race, creed or color.'"

Aside from the ethical questions the practice raises, profiling aimed at Muslims isn't always accurate or knowledgeable. For example, many Sikhs—followers of the Sikhism religion—are stopped by agents and officers who mistake them for Muslims. Most Sikhs are of Indian descent. As part of their faith, many Sikh men wear turbans and many women wear headscarves. TSA agents and others sometimes confuse these head coverings with those worn by Muslims and target Sikhs for extra screening and monitoring. In general, people with dark skin are also singled out for heightened scrutiny, even though Muslims do not necessarily have dark skin. An anonymous, white TSA officer at Logan International Airport in Boston, Massachusetts, says of his fellow airport security officers, "They just pull aside anyone who they don't like the way they look—if they are black and have expensive clothes or jewelry, or if they are Hispanic."

By contrast, Khalid El Khatib, a light-skinned Palestinian American who is Muslim, notes that while he frequently undergoes extra screening at airports, TSA personnel "are quick to admit that it's likely because of my name and often acknowledge it's unfair. I can't help but feel this [apologetic attitude] is because of my whiteness, the sameness I share with these airport workers. I can't imagine a gate agent would tell my father, with his accent and thick black mustache, that they're sorry—that he probably doesn't deserve the extra hassle."

Terrorist Watch Lists

Besides scrutinizing Middle Eastern travelers in general, the DHS maintains numerous terrorist watch lists. In 2004 the DHS launched Operation Front Line, a classified program that aims to identify possible terrorists by investigating more than twenty-five hundred foreigners living in the United States. DHS officials questioned foreigners from a range of Middle Eastern nations about their religious practices, their feelings about the United States, and whether they had access to biological or chemical weapons. The DHS stated that the targets of these investigations were identified "without regard to race, ethnicity or religion." However, records revealed that 79 percent of the people investigated came from nations with majority Muslim populations. Furthermore, very few targets of the investigation were ultimately charged with any crime. Those who did face charges were typically accused of immigration violations but not of posing threats to national

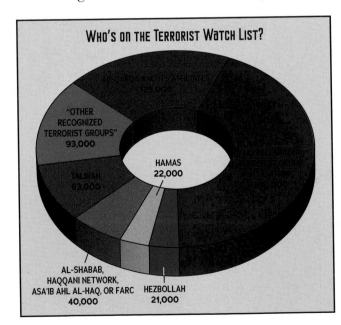

WHO'S ON THE TERRORIST WATCH LIST?

AL-QAEDA AND ITS AFFILIATES
128,000

"OTHER RECOGNIZED TERRORIST GROUPS"
93,000

TALIBAN
63,000

HAMAS
22,000

AL-SHABAB, HAQQANI NETWORK, ASA'IB AHL AL-HAQ, OR FARC
40,000

HEZBOLLAH
21,000

In 2014 the online publication the *Intercept* obtained classified government documents related to the US government's confidential Terrorist Screening Database. According to the *Intercept*'s analysis of these documents, this database of terrorist suspects includes more than 650,000 people, of whom nearly one-half have no known connections to established terrorist groups.

security. An analysis by the National Litigation Project at Yale Law School concluded that as a tool to identify likely terrorists, the program was an expensive, time-consuming failure.

The most notorious DHS list is the highly confidential no-fly list. It is believed to name tens of thousands of people—including hundreds of American citizens—who are not permitted to fly into or out of the United States. Many have committed no crimes. Most have no idea their names are on this list. And most are of Arab descent.

ARE YOU ON A TERRORIST WATCH LIST?

Officials at the Department of Homeland Security or the FBI can place individuals on a terrorist watch list if they raise reasonable suspicion based on any of the following factors:

- traveling to or from a country with ties to terrorism

- being reported by someone else

- being "representative" of a terrorist group

- being related to, an associate of, or an alleged acquaintance of a known or suspected terrorist

- falling into a "category of individuals" determined by DHS to be a threat

- posting content that raises "reasonable suspicion" of terrorist connections on social media sites (in combination with at least one other factor; this content alone is not sufficient to qualify someone to be on a watch list)

- processing errors, such as filling out forms incorrectly, by DHS officials

Official guidelines for the watch lists are extremely confidential and are not available to the public, but investigative journalists have obtained DHS and FBI documents that shed light on the system.

One person on the no-fly list, Saeb Mokdad, is a businessperson of Lebanese origin. Mokdad had never been convicted of a crime, and he has been a US citizen since 1991. Nevertheless, Mokdad was prevented from flying to Lebanon three times and came to suspect that he was on the no-fly list. (Some of his Lebanese relatives had been involved in several kidnappings, which Mokdad suspects triggered his inclusion on the list.) In 2012 Mokdad contacted the DHS. The department neither confirmed nor denied that he was on the no-fly list but "determined that no changes or corrections are warranted at this time." In 2013 Mokdad filed a civil case against the US attorney general, the FBI director, and the Terrorist Screening Center (TSC) director, challenging his inclusion on the list. The Arab-American Civil Rights League (ACRL) represented Mokdad. His case is still undecided.

Meanwhile, a court of appeals ruled in 2015 that lower courts could hear similar cases challenging the no-fly list. This would allow more people to have their cases heard more easily. ACRL civil rights attorney Nabih Ayad praised the decision as a step forward for Muslims, Arabs, and others of Middle Eastern descent whom the government has deemed suspicious based on racial profiling. "This ruling confirms what we at the ACRL have stated from day one—that the unwarranted and unconstitutional profiling of an entire group of people simply based on their ethnicity must be struck down as a violation of this nation's highest law: the Constitution."

A Ban on Muslims?

In 2015 and 2016, American fear and anger toward Muslims spiked again after Islamist terrorists carried out coordinated attacks in France, Belgium, and the United States. The attacks coincided with an ongoing refugee crisis, as millions of people—most of whom are Muslims—fled the war-torn Middle Eastern nation of Syria. Governors of several states declared that their states would not receive any more Syrian refugees for the time being. Republican US presidential candidate Donald Trump called for further measures, such as shutting down mosques in the United States, blocking all Muslims from entering the country, and setting up a database to register and track Muslims already in the United States.

Other influential figures on both sides of the political aisle endorsed at least some monitoring of Muslims. Businessperson Haim Saban, a major contributor to the campaign of Democratic presidential candidate Hillary Clinton, said, "The reality is that certain things that are unacceptable in times of peace—such as profiling, listening in on anyone and everybody who looks suspicious, or interviewing Muslims in a more intense way than interviewing Christian refugees—[are] all acceptable [during war]. Why? Because we value life more than our civil liberties."

Other Americans disagreed. After a June 2016 mass shooting at a gay nightclub in Orlando, Florida, carried out by a US citizen who was a nonpracticing Muslim, resurgence of anti-Muslim sentiment among civilians and politicians intensified. Communities of color and civil rights advocacy groups condemned these reactions. One group, the National Queer Asian Pacific Islander Alliance (NQAPIA), said in a statement, "Furthering such rhetoric will only lead to more policies that normalize surveillance of and violence against APIs [Asian and Pacific Islanders] and other communities of color. . . . NQAPIA advocates firmly against policies that profile and instill fear in our communities."

Demonstrators in Los Angeles block traffic to protest racial profiling and police brutality. Protesters use raised hands, often combined with the mantra "Hands up, don't shoot," to invoke **police** killings of people of color.

CHAPTER 6
CALLS FOR CHANGE

In 2013 Trayon Christian, an eighteen-year-old college student, went shopping in New York City. He visited the high-end department store Barneys, where he bought a designer belt with his debit card. At the clerk's request, he showed his ID. But a few minutes after he left the store with his purchase, two undercover police officers stopped him on the street. Christian says they asked to see his ID and look in his shopping bag, claiming that someone at Barneys had been concerned that Christian had used a fake debit card. "The detectives were asking me, 'How could you afford a belt like this? Where did you get this money from?'" Christian recalled. The officers then arrested him, handcuffing him and taking him to the police station. Police released him about two hours later without pressing charges. Christian was outraged by both the NYPD's behavior and the store clerk's suspicions. "I brought the belt back to Barneys a few days later and returned it. I got my money back, I'm not shopping there again," he said. "It's cruel. It's racist." He went on to file a lawsuit against Barneys, accusing the company of racial discrimination and profiling. In 2016 Barneys settled the lawsuit by agreeing to pay Christian $45,000. As Christian's attorney, Michael Palillo, put it, "His only crime was being a young black guy buying a $300 belt."

Demanding Reforms

Trayon Christian refused to accept racial profiling as an inevitable inconvenience and humiliation. Instead, he spoke out against his treatment and took action to prevent similar incidents from happening to others. Like Christian, many Americans are challenging the use of racial profiling by both private citizens and law enforcement. A 2015 poll by the Leadership Conference on Civil and Human Rights found that 57 percent of Americans support a ban on racial profiling by police and national security agencies (such as the FBI, the DHS, and US Immigration and Customs Enforcement). Elected officials, lawmakers, advocacy groups, and other concerned citizens are promoting public awareness of racial

SHOPPING WHILE . . .

Besides Barneys, other high-profile retailers accused of racial bias include Macy's flagship store in New York City, which was investigated in 2005 and 2013 for disproportionate stops of black and Hispanic shoppers; the pharmacy chain CVS, which former employees sued in 2015 on charges of directing workers to profile black and Hispanic customers; and fashion retailer Zara, which, according to a 2015 report, identified black and Hispanic customers as potential shoplifters much more often than white shoppers.

profiling and pursuing changes to the systems that support the practice.

At the national level, the DOJ announced in 2014 that it would enact new, stricter policies for federal law enforcement agencies (with exceptions for the FBI and US Border Patrol) with the goal of reducing racial profiling in the United States. Then attorney general Eric Holder noted, "I have repeatedly made clear that racial profiling by law enforcement is not only wrong, it is misguided and ineffective—because it can mistakenly focus investigative efforts, waste precious resources and, ultimately, undermine the public trust."

Another proposed reform is the End Racial Profiling Act (ERPA), a bill introduced by Democratic legislators in the US House of Representatives and the US Senate on April 22, 2015. (The bill had been previously introduced in 2004, 2005, 2007, 2009, 2010, 2011, and 2013 but failed to gain traction.) If approved by Congress and signed into law by the president, ERPA would outlaw racial profiling by all law enforcement officials, from city police to federal agents. One of the senators who presented the ERPA legislation, Democrat Ben Cardin of Maryland, spoke to Congress about the negative impact of profiling, saying: "While the vast majority of law enforcement work with professionalism and fidelity to the rule of law, we can never accept the outright targeting of individuals based on the way they look or dress. As a matter of practice, racial profiling just doesn't work and it erodes the trust that is necessary between law enforcement and the very communities they protect."

At the state level, reforms focus on enforcing existing anti-profiling laws through increased standards of transparency and accountability for police departments. In late 2014, the

NAACP reported that twenty US states do not have laws that explicitly ban racial profiling. Of the thirty states that do prohibit profiling, none have provisions that are specific or extensive enough to meet the NAACP's standards. In 2015 a few states moved to toughen their anti-profiling laws. For instance, in August 2015, Maryland expanded its anti-profiling law, which bans racial profiling at traffic stops. The state's attorney general, Brian E. Frosh, issued new guidelines that prohibit the use of race or ethnicity as a factor in any police decisions—not just traffic stops—and prohibit profiling based on other identifying factors such as national origin and religion. In October 2015, California governor Jerry Brown signed into law the Racial and Identity Profiling Act.

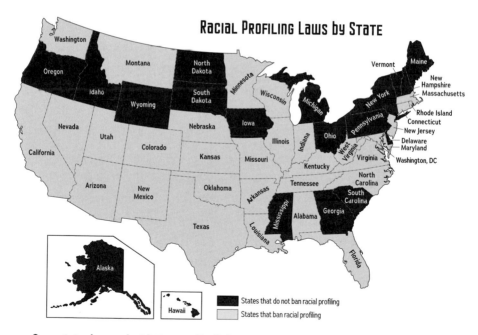

Racial Profiling Laws by State

- States that do not ban racial profiling
- States that ban racial profiling

Some states have no legislation specifically banning racial profiling by law enforcement. Other states ban the practice in broad terms but offer few guidelines for what qualifies as an instance of profiling. Consequences for illegal profiling also vary on a state-by-state basis.

The law requires California law enforcement officials to consistently report information on every stop they make—including the race of the person stopped and what charges or other actions, if any, resulted from the stop. Opponents of the law say the data will be of little use, as it won't provide any objective insight into what officers are thinking as they conduct stops. Furthermore, some dislike the idea of encouraging officers to pay attention to race. "If you think about it, this bill actually encourages racial profiling by requiring officers to report what they perceive to be the race, ethnicity, gender and age of the person they stopped," says Roger Mayberry, president of the California Fraternal Order of Police.

Advocates, on the other hand, say this data will provide statistical evidence of where profiling is happening and how pervasive it is, paving the way for reforms. Conversely, data that indicates equitable treatment of citizens will reinforce police departments' claims of impartiality, notes David Harris, a scholar of police behavior at Pittsburgh University School of Law. Data that shows no evidence of racial profiling "enables the police department to say to the public, look, we looked at the data and no, we don't have this problem."

In Arizona, Latino activists are pushing for similar legislation. "We want data," says Phoenix-based anti-profiling advocate DeeDee Garcia Blasé. "We want statistics. We want to hold the Phoenix Police Department, the Maricopa County Sheriff's [Office], all the local law enforcement agencies accountable."

Individual cities are also implementing changes. In June 2016, in response to public outcry over police shootings of black citizens, Chicago leaders introduced a groundbreaking policy shift. Chicago became the largest city in the country to adopt a policy for publicly releasing video footage of police

"I liked my job [as a police officer], and I was good at it.

"But more and more, I felt like I couldn't do the work I set out to do. I was participating in a profoundly corrupt criminal justice system. I could not, in good conscience, participate in a system that was so intentionally unfair and racist. So after five years on the job, I quit.

"Unfortunately, I don't think better training alone will reduce police brutality. My fellow officers and I took plenty of classes on racial sensitivity and on limiting the use of force.

"The problem is that cops aren't held accountable for their actions, and they know it. These officers violate rights with impunity [no consequences]. They know there's a different criminal justice system for civilians and police. . . . We could start to change that by mandating that a special prosecutor be appointed to try excessive force cases. And we need more independent oversight, with teeth. I have little confidence in internal investigations.

"The number of people in uniform who will knowingly and maliciously violate your human rights is huge. . . . We have a lot of work to do."

—Redditt Hudson, NAACP employee and former police officer, 2014

shootings and other excessive force incidents. Footage must be released within sixty days of an incident, a sweeping change in a city known for the distrust between police and citizens of color. Local anti-profiling and anti-police-brutality advocates praised the policy as a step toward rebuilding public confidence in the police department. Some think the policy could serve as a blueprint for other cities around the country.

Activists urge police departments to require on-duty officers to wear body cameras that record stops, arrests, and other actions. Like cell phone videos taken by bystanders, body cameras have brought clarity to some cases that involve conflicting testimony. One case that highlighted the potential impact of body cameras was that of Samuel DuBose. On July 19, 2015, University of Cincinnati police officer Ray Tensing pulled over Samuel DuBose for a missing front license plate. During the course of the traffic stop, after DuBose failed to find his driver's license, Tensing started to open the car door, telling DuBose to step out. DuBose instead closed his door and started the car. Tensing then shot DuBose in the head, killing him. Afterward, Tensing said that he had fired because he felt he was in danger of being run over by DuBose's car and believed his own life was at risk.

Footage from Tensing's body camera revealed that while DuBose did close his door, his car had barely moved when Tensing shot him. DuBose's hands were visible, and Tensing appeared to face no threat to his life. After viewing the footage, Joe Deters, the prosecuting attorney for Hamilton County, Ohio, remarked, "This office has probably reviewed 100 police shootings, and this is the first time we've thought, 'This is without question a murder.'" An investigatory report also stated that while DuBose was in the wrong when he closed the car door, "Tensing set in motion the fatal chain of events that led to the death of DuBose." Ultimately, Tensing was fired from his job and charged with murder. The footage from his body camera was the key to both of those decisions.

Sensitivity and bias training is another way individual police departments can address racial profiling issues. In 2014, for example, the Omaha Police Department in Nebraska began implementing a training program that helps officers recognize and reduce their unconscious biases. "Profiling is something that won't be tolerated," says Omaha police chief

Todd Schmaderer. "We take complaints very seriously." The move drew praise from the ACLU of Nebraska, whose director, Danielle Conrad, said, "This is the exact kind of training we have been advocating for." Dozens of other police departments across the nation have adopted similar training programs, which use role playing and group discussions to address implicit bias.

In addition to police reforms, activists have pushed for sweeping changes at all levels of the criminal justice system. To address racial disparities in sentencing and incarceration rates, advocates call for more community-based alternatives to incarceration; educational opportunities and mental health support for inmates to improve their chances of reintegrating into society after release; and the early release of inmates who have committed nonviolent, low-level crimes. One step toward reform came in 2010, when the US Congress passed the Fair Sentencing Act (FSA). The law shortened mandatory minimum sentences for crack cocaine offenses, which disproportionately affect people of color. Numerous advocacy groups urge the federal government to reduce the sentences of prisoners already serving time for these offenses. According to Marc Mauer, the executive director of the criminal justice nonprofit group the Sentencing Project, "The challenge for both policy makers and the public is to build on these developments and to think creatively about ways of enhancing both public safety and racial justice."

Taking to the Streets

Along with political and legal initiatives, independent organizations and individuals are working to combat racial profiling and racism. While not all of these groups and

TAKING ON THE TSA

In 2012 the Sikh Coalition and other civil rights groups created a mobile app to combat racial profiling by the TSA. People could use the app to report incidents in which they believed they had been profiled at US airports. Called FlyRights, the app helps travelers know their rights, file profiling complaints against the TSA, and share information with other users. Other groups are also keeping a close eye on the TSA's practices. For instance, in April 2016, Andrew Rhoades, an assistant federal security director for the TSA in Minnesota, reported a troubling exchange with his supervisor. The supervisor had asked Rhoades to provide the agency's field intelligence officer with the names of Somali Americans who visited his office. These people would be screened for terrorist connections before being permitted to enter TSA offices. "With our current world affairs . . . we need to be mindful of those we interact with," the supervisor told Rhoades. Since Rhoades had never been asked to take this step for any other group of people, he felt that his supervisor's instructions amounted to racial profiling.

Rhoades alerted national TSA and DHS authorities. While the TSA promised to review the complaint, Minneapolis's Muslim community mobilized to demand further action. Jaylani Hussein, a Somali American who heads Minnesota's chapter of the Council on American-Islamic Relations, asked the DHS's inspector general to investigate the incident. Muslim community members spoke out about incidents of profiling by TSA employees and called for TSA policy reforms. Local Muslim groups received support from the local Black Lives Matter chapter as well as from US

representative Keith Ellison of Minnesota, *shown right in a 2007 photo,* (the first Muslim American elected to the US Congress). Somali American community leader Sadik Warfa summed up the coalition's goals in saying, "We must show we will not tolerate anti-Muslim discrimination."

individuals are focusing exclusively on ending racial profiling itself, they share the goals of recognizing and lessening prejudice and discrimination in the United States.

The 2012 killing of seventeen-year-old Trayvon Martin sparked widespread sorrow and anger across the nation. The violent deaths of other people of color, including Eric Garner, Michael Brown, and Freddie Gray, prompted more Americans to speak out against racial profiling. Citizens expressed their outrage through demonstrations. For instance, after the announcement that no police officers would be indicted in the 2014 case of Eric Garner, thousands of protesters marched in New York City, chanting "No justice, no peace, no racist police" and "I can't breathe." In South Carolina, following Walter Scott's death at the hands of police officer, protesters gathered outside the North Charleston City Hall, carrying signs with messages such as "The whole world is watching" and "Back turned don't shoot."

Also in 2014, protests erupted across Saint Louis after Michael Brown's death, setting off months of on-and-off unrest that ranged from peaceful demonstrations to riots, looting, and vandalism. Police responded by using tear gas and smoke against crowds. Unrest spiked again when a grand jury chose not to indict Officer Darren Wilson, the man who had shot Brown. Brown's family asked for calm, saying, "We are profoundly disappointed that the killer of our child will not face the consequence of his actions. While we understand that many others share our pain, we ask that you channel your frustration in ways that will make a positive change. We need to work together to fix the system that allowed this to happen."

Similarly, in the wake of Freddie Gray's 2015 death in Baltimore, demonstrators marched through the streets, protesters clashed with riot police, and buildings and vehicles were damaged. Marilyn Mosby, the state's attorney for Baltimore, addressed the turmoil that had rocked Baltimore and called on protesters to act peacefully, saying, "I will seek justice on your behalf. This is a moment. This is your moment. Let's ensure that we have peaceful and productive rallies that will develop structural and systemic changes for generations to come. You're at the forefront of this cause."

Many observers expressed disapproval at the conduct of protesters, asking why African Americans were "destroying their own communities." Describing the unrest in Ferguson, *Chicago Tribune* columnist John Kass wrote, "Buildings burned . . . and others were broken into and robbed. Shops were looted by gangs bent on mayhem, the crowds running into the stores, some of the shops with signs that told the looters these were black-owned businesses. But that didn't stop those who came to take, and you could see them running out again with goods in their arms, giggling and shrieking as they celebrated their wild spree."

Others insisted that most protesters were peaceful and that the actions of a few should not distract Americans from the larger issues. "It seems far easier to focus on the few looters who have reacted unproductively to this tragedy than to focus on the killing of Michael Brown," noted Brittney Cooper, a professor of Africana studies at Rutgers University in New Jersey. "No, I don't support looting. But I question a society that always sees the product of the provocation and never the provocation itself. I question a society that values property over black life." Some noted too that stereotypes of African Americans as violent and irrational were once more at work, underpinning certain criticisms of the protests. White rioters

An NYPD officer arrests a demonstrator at a 2015 march in New York City to protest police killings of unarmed citizens.

throughout US history tend to be perceived very differently from people of color who riot. "From the Boston Tea Party to Shays' Rebellion, riots made America, for better or worse," points out activist Robert Stephens II. For Stephens and other protesters, the larger goal "is to transition outrage and disruption into constructive political organization."

Other observers contended that news coverage of these incidents reveals another facet of persistent, often subconscious racial bias. From local TV stations to national newspapers, media outlets have drawn criticism for presenting incidents of unrest differently depending on who is involved. According to critics, if the people in question are not white, media coverage tends to portray them as aggressive, dangerous, destructive, and criminal. By contrast, if the perpetrators are white, their actions are more likely to be presented as nonthreatening rowdiness and mischief (as were the actions among white college students in New Hampshire in October 2014). Or may describe them as courageous stands for a principle (as were the tactics of armed white demonstrators who occupied an Oregon wildlife refuge in January 2016 to protest federal government control of public land).

Similarly, some observers point out that race plays a role in what major papers, websites, and other media outlets choose not to report as news. For instance, during and after the Baltimore protests, many African Americans called for calm, worked to defuse tensions, protected property, and helped clean up the streets. These peaceful actions, however, were not covered as widely as reports on violence and destruction. Twitter users and others highlighted these disparities in coverage, using them as starting points for discussions about racial stereotypes.

Strength in Numbers

One of the largest and most vocal organizations speaking out against racism and racial profiling is Black Lives Matter (BLM). Formed in 2012 after Trayvon Martin's death, this group has chapters all over the United States and describes its mission as "a call to action and a response to the virulent anti-Black racism that permeates our society." Across the nation, numerous other advocacy groups for people of color have aligned themselves with the BLM movement. These groups have organized protests and demonstrations to raise awareness of racism, racial profiling, and police misconduct against people of color. For instance, groups have staged "die-ins" where protesters gather in busy public spaces—such as shopping malls, streets, and train or subway stations—and lie down on the ground or floor as though dead, a form of respect for victims of deadly profiling incidents. These dramatic demonstrations often intentionally interfere with everyday activities such as commutes and commerce as a way of drawing attention to the protesters' cause.

Many anti-profiling demonstrations have adopted a variety of symbols and slogans that draw on past events in powerful and emotional ways. In July 2014, in response to Eric Garner's death after a police officer used an illegal choke hold on him, Garner's last words—"I Can't Breathe"—became a mantra. The phrase appeared on shirts, banners, signs, and more. In December 2014, several prominent professional basketball players, including LeBron James and Kobe Bryant, attended pregame practices wearing T-shirts with the words "I Can't Breathe." That same month, high school basketball players at a school in California were told they wouldn't be allowed to take part in a tournament after members of the girls' squad wore "I Can't Breathe" T-shirts during warm-ups.

Similarly, after the August 2014 killing of Michael Brown, the words "Hands Up, Don't Shoot" spread quickly. The eventual investigation into Brown's killing reported that Brown probably did not say "hands up" or raise his hands in surrender before he was shot. Nevertheless, for protesters and others, the words remained symbolic of the many unarmed black men killed by officers of the law. As Hakeem Jeffries, a New York member of the US House of Representatives, put it, "'Hands up, don't shoot,' is a rallying cry of people all across America who are fed up with police violence . . . in Ferguson, in Brooklyn, in Cleveland, in Oakland, in cities and counties and rural communities."

Concerned citizens also make powerful use of social media. Posts by "Black Twitter," an unofficial group of thousands of black Twitter users, call attention to specific incidents and foster larger conversations about racial discrimination and bias. For example, in the wake of Sandra Bland's death, users adopted the hashtag #IfIDieInPoliceCustody, contending that police officers often lie about the circumstances of such deaths. Tweets included "#IfIDieInPoliceCustody I did not commit suicide, I did not resist arrest or be combative. I didn't go for the taser or gun" and "#IfIDieInPoliceCustody know that they killed me. I would do everything in my power to get home to my family. So never stop questioning." Activists and their allies use social media as a way of directly speaking to figures in power, from police chiefs to politicians. They have called for investigations into suspicious deaths and have lobbied legislators to change or introduce laws to prevent profiling.

Hoping to create change on a wider scale, reformers have carried their message to political campaigns at all levels. For instance, after seventeen-year-old Laquan McDonald died at the hands of Chicago police officer Jason Van Dyke in October 2014, local civil rights advocates strongly criticized Cook County state's attorney Anita Alvarez, who delayed pressing charges against the officers until more than a year after Laquan's death. Citizens' groups used social media and public demonstrations to call attention to Alvarez's record, noting that over a seven-year period she had chosen not to file charges against police officers in more than sixty-eight cases of fatal shootings. A coalition of Chicago civil rights groups vocally opposed her candidacy in the county's 2016 Democratic primary election for state's attorney. Observers in the media credited these groups with Alvarez's defeat by opponent Kim Foxx.

In Ohio, BLM and affiliated organizations achieved a similar primary victory with the defeat of Cuyahoga County

"The argument is that [Michael Brown's death] is not a perfect case, because Brown—and, one would assume, now [Eric] Garner— isn't a perfect victim and the protesters haven't all been perfectly civil, so therefore any movement to counter black oppression that flows from the case is inherently flawed. But this is ridiculous and reductive, because it fails to acknowledge that the whole system is imperfect and rife with flaws. We don't need to identify angels and demons to understand that inequity is hell."

—Charles M. Blow, African American *New York Times* columnist, 2014

prosecutor Timothy McGinty, who had controversially recommended that no charges be filed against Cleveland police officers in the November 2014 death of Tamir Rice. "These two elections show the growing influence of the Black Lives Matter movement," stated the *New York Times* editorial board. "Two young people were gunned down, and the voters in those grieving communities were not going to let the prosecutors off the hook."

At the national level, BLM activists worked to advance their agenda throughout the 2016 presidential race. Rather than endorsing a candidate, activists declared their determination to hold all candidates accountable for their policies and attitudes related to racial inequality. In addition to arranging private meetings with Democratic candidates Hillary Clinton and Bernie Sanders, BLM demonstrators became a vocal presence at rallies for candidates of both parties. For instance, at a 2015 town hall gathering for Sanders and rival Democratic candidate Martin O'Malley, dozens of demonstrators demanded that the candidates address concerns about racial inequality. Tia Oso of the Black Alliance for Just Immigration climbed onstage and spoke to the candidates, asking a question that encapsulated the BLM mission: "As the leader of this nation, will you advance a racial justice agenda that will dismantle—not reform, not make progress—but will begin to dismantle structural racism in the United States?" On this occasion, Sanders and O'Malley were relatively receptive to the protesters. The response at other events has ranged from combative (as when former president Bill Clinton, husband of presidential candidate Hillary Clinton, responded defensively to a BLM critic at a 2016 rally) to violent. For example, demonstrators encountered verbal and physical abuse from audience members and security staff at rallies for Republican presidential candidate Donald Trump.

Critics contend that Black Lives Matter and its allies promote irrationally destructive behavior and negative attitudes. In response to accusations that they are "too angry," or "too aggressive," BLM activists say that this perspective leans on racial stereotypes and that their anger is not only justified but necessary to achieve progress. "White rage doesn't have to take to the streets and face rubber bullets to be heard," says Carol Anderson, associate professor of African American studies at Emory University in Georgia. "Instead, white rage carries an aura of respectability and has access to the courts, police, legislatures and governors."

Many critics of BLM also argue that the core message of Black Lives Matter is divisive and unproductive and that it inaccurately makes every incident into a conversation about race. Some suggest that a more acceptable slogan would be "All Lives Matter." BLM activists and supporters insist that this perspective willfully ignores an uncomfortable truth about racial bias in the United States. As journalist Joshua Adams puts it, "a Black person's life should matter as much as anyone else's," and yet "in this country's past and present, Black life hasn't been treated as if it matters."

Individual Voices

People of all backgrounds can contribute to the conversation about racial profiling and racial inequality in the United States. A simple first step is to take an assessment known as a hidden bias test. These tests are designed to help people of all backgrounds become aware of unconscious stereotypes or prejudices that may influence their thoughts and actions. One organization that encourages the use of these tests is Teaching Tolerance, a group founded by a civil rights advocacy organization called the Southern Poverty Law Center, based in Alabama. The organization's website explains,

"Your willingness to examine your own possible biases is an important step in understanding the roots of stereotypes and prejudice in our society." One such test was developed by Project Implicit, an organization started by psychologists at the University of Virginia, the University of Washington, and Harvard University. Project Implicit's tests measure unconscious biases based on race, as well as on gender and sexual orientation. The educational website Understanding Prejudice offers similar tests. Similarly, you can consider if and when you might display microaggressions. Many websites, including the blog *Microaggressions.com*, offer examples of microaggressions and what they can mean.

Understanding your own biases can help you recognize and resist their influence on your behavior and sense of self. "The good news is, you can control it once you think about it," says Maxine Williams, the global director of diversity at Facebook. "If, at every [move], you're checking yourself—'Hold on, am I

David O'Neal Brown, the chief of the Dallas Police Department, grew up fearing and avoiding police officers in his neighborhood. Yet he joined the police force in the 1980s, hoping to help fight the crack cocaine epidemic that had devastated many families he knew. Soon after he became police chief in 2010, his son killed a police officer in an altercation and was then fatally shot by other officers. Brown has promoted de-escalation training for police officers and emphasized the need for officers to build positive relationships with community members.

WHITE ALLIES IN THE ANTI-PROFILING MOVEMENT

While people of color are at the forefront of the fight against racial profiling, many white Americans identify as allies of the movement. Allies have joined protests, vigils, and demonstrations; called on lawmakers for improved legislation; participated in social media discussions about racial issues; and collaborated with people of color in their communities. For instance, pastors at predominantly white churches have publicly proclaimed solidarity with Black Lives Matter.

In their daily lives, white allies can strive to be more aware of racism, to speak out against it, and to create space for people of color to express their points of view. Workers can advocate for more racial diversity in their workplaces and for workplace policies that are inclusive and respectful of people of color. Americans can have conversations with friends and family members about racially biased perceptions. Professor Brittney Cooper of Rutgers University in New Jersey advises white allies to focus on spreading awareness among fellow white Americans and to "use their privilege to confront racial injustices when they see them happening, whether in the grocery store or the boardroom." African American writer and professor Roxane Gay urges white allies to "Actively listen when marginalized people tell you about their oppression—don't offer your pity (which only helps you) and don't apologize. Listen and do your best to understand what it feels like to live with oppression as a constant. Speak up when you hear people making racist jokes. Speak up when you see injustice in action. Inform yourself about your local law enforcement and how they treat people of color. Vote. Take a stand."

objectively evaluating these people?'—you're less likely to make those mistakes. . . . Keep yourself accountable by checking yourself, and keep others accountable."

You can also speak up about the related issues, events, and causes that matter to you. One way of doing this is by sharing views on social media or through a blog. You might write a letter to the editor of a local newspaper, write articles for your school newspaper, help organize school and community events to raise awareness about certain issues, or join organizations that support related causes. Support and participate in interracial dialogue and events at your school. You can also support leaders and candidates who share your views, even if you are not yet old enough to vote.

Americans of every age, race, and ethnic background can play a role in the struggle to combat racial profiling in the

WHAT CAN YOU DO?

Young people can participate in the struggle against racial profiling and the movement for racial equity in a variety of ways, including the following:

- Share information, personal experiences (yours and others'), and calls to action on social media.

- E-mail, call, write to, or tweet to your representatives at the local, state, and federal level urging them to champion reforms.

- Attend or help organize a "know your rights" training to prepare people for dealing with discrimination from law enforcement and others.

- Attend anti-profiling events such as rallies and marches, or deliver supplies (such as food, weather accessories, or medical supplies) to demonstrators.

- Volunteer for a local organization that supports the causes you believe in. Make phone calls or send e-mails to potential supporters, do data entry, help maintain the organization's website, or help create posters and flyers for events.

- Discuss issues of racial profiling, discrimination, and injustice with family members, friends, and peers.

- At school, report instances of racial discrimination to a teacher or to the principal.

United States. As more people—especially young people—become involved, many advocates for equity and justice see reason for hope. Activist and poet Jeremey Johnson says, "Voices that have gone unheard and unrecognized in previous years are now being heard and will no longer be ignored. . . . As long as there are racist systems, there will be a movement of youth visibly and vocally advocating for their civil rights. This is just the beginning."

- At work, report instances of racial discrimination to management. If your supervisor doesn't address the problem, you can file a formal complaint with your company.

- If you notice someone being harassed in public, alert an authority figure—such as a bus driver or a store manager. If it's safe to do so, help the targeted person move away from the confrontational person.

- Report possible hate crimes to the police.

- If you or someone you know experiences discrimination from police officers, work with trusted adults to explore your options to address the issue. Consult the ACLU website for resources.

- When you are old enough, register to vote and research candidates for local, state, and federal office. Campaign and vote for candidates who support your beliefs and goals.

- Continually educate yourself by reading about racial profiling issues and listening to others' stories. Continually work against your own biases to avoid profiling or discriminating against others.

- Consider pursuing a future career that will contribute to social justice. Some possibilities include working as a civil rights attorney, a police officer, a nonprofit employee, and a developer of software and other technology that can track and combat cases of racial profiling.

Glossary

acquit: to free a person from a criminal charge by a not guilty verdict

Arab: a member of the Arabic-speaking peoples who have historic roots in the Arabian Peninsula and who live mostly in the Middle East

bias: a personal opinion in favor of or against a person or group, usually in a way considered to be unfair or unfounded. The opinion can be explicit (deliberate and obvious) or implicit (subtle or unconscious).

cabinet: the most senior appointed officers of the executive branch of the US federal government

discrimination: the unequal treatment of different groups of people, especially due to race, religion, gender, or sexual orientation

disproportionate: an unreasonable difference; too large or small compared to a related measurement

equality: fairness based on treating all people the same way

equity: fairness based on giving additional aid or opportunity to people who are disadvantaged by historic and systemic injustices

gerrymandering: the process of manipulating the boundaries of electoral districts to favor a political party or class, often resulting in districts of widely varying size and shape

grand jury: a group, usually made up of twenty-three people, assembled to examine the validity of an accusation before a case goes to trial

hate crime: a crime that is motivated by racial, sexual, or other prejudice and typically involves violence

hijab: a veil or scarf that covers the head and chest, worn by many Muslim women. In some Muslim traditions, hijab refers to an entire outfit covering most of a woman's body.

Hispanic: of or relating to Spanish-speaking countries, especially those of Latin America. In the United States, Hispanic is often used interchangeably with Latino, Latina, or the gender-neutral Latinx.

indict: to formally charge someone with a crime

infrastructure: the organizational structures, resources, and facilities—such as buildings, roads, and power supplies—needed for the operation of a business, a community, or a society

institutional racism: a pattern of social institutions—including government organizations, schools, banks, and courts of law—treating a group of people unfairly based on their race

Islam: a major world religion founded in 610 CE by the prophet Muhammad in what is now Saudi Arabia

Islamist: a follower of the political ideology of Islamism, which calls for a government that follows an extremely conservative interpretation of Islam

Islamophobia: irrational fear of all Muslims, rooted in the unsubstantiated belief that the religion of Islam inherently promotes violence and hatred of Westerners

Latino: of Latin American origin or descent. The term Latina may refer to a woman or girl. Sometimes the gender-neutral term Latinx is used.

lynch: to kill someone, especially by hanging, for an alleged offense without a legal trial. Historically, black Americans have been the main victims of lynching.

Middle East: a region comprised of southwestern Asia and northeastern Africa that is home to many groups, including Arabs

mosque: a Muslim place of worship

Muslim: a follower of the religion of Islam

net worth: the total monetary value of a person, family, or company after subtracting any debts

police brutality: the use of excessive force—such as the physical abuse or killing of a civilian—by law enforcement officers

prejudice: a preconceived opinion that is based on emotion, not on reality, experience, or reason

racism: the belief that all members of a race possess characteristics or abilities specific to that race, usually linked to the belief that one's own race is superior to another

redlining: the practice of marking neighborhoods with populations of color as "red" areas whose residents are ineligible for home loans. The policy was officially used by the Federal Housing Administration and private mortgage companies between 1934 and 1968 to exclude black Americans.

second-degree murder: a killing carried out with hatred, ill will, or spite but not planned ahead of time

stereotype: a widely held but often unfair and untrue belief about a type of person or thing

Source Notes

4 *Los Angeles Times* staff, "Hear the 911 Call about Tamir Rice: Gun Is 'Probably Fake,' Caller Says," *Los Angeles Times* video, 0:15–0:1:45, November 26, 2014, http://www.latimes.com/nation/nationnow/la-na-nn-tamir-rice-911-call-20141126-htmlstory.html.

5 Lauren Gambino, "Tami Rice Shooting: Cleveland Police Handcuffed Sister as 12-Year-Old Lay Dying," *Guardian* (US ed.), January 8, 2015, http://www.theguardian.com/us-news/2015/jan/08/cleveland-police-handcuffed-sister-tamir-rice-lay-dying-video.

6 Perry Bacon Jr., "Tamir Rice Decision Illustrates Power and Limits of 'Black Lives' Movement, *NBC News*, December 29, 2015, http://www.nbcnews.com/meet-the-press/tamir-rice-decision-illustrates-power-limits-black-lives-movement-n487106.

6 "Racial Profiling: Definition," ACLU, accessed October 2, 2015, https://www.aclu.org/racial-profiling-definition.

6 Amnesty International USA, "Threat and Humiliation: Racial Profiling, Domestic Security, and Human Rights in the United States," accessed October 2, 2015, available online at http://www.amnestyusa.org/pdfs/rp_report.pdf.

8 Kim Christensen and Matt Hamilton, "California's Racial Profiling Law Is 'Terrible' Legislation, Police Officials Say," *Los Angeles Times*, October 4, 2015, http://www.latimes.com/local/crime/la-me-brown-reax-20151005-story.html.

8 Jack Glaser, *Suspect Race: Causes and Consequences of Racial Profiling* (New York: Oxford University Press, 2015), 17.

8–9 "Racial Profiling," ACLU, accessed October 2, 2015, https://www.aclu.org/issues/racial-justice/race-and-criminal-justice/racial-profiling.

11 Sonya Sotomayor, "Supreme Court of the United States, No. 12-682, Schuette, Attorney General of Michigan, v. Coalition to Defend Affirmative Action, Integration and Immigrant Rights and Fight for Equality by Any Means Necessary (BAMN), et. al.," 45–46, decided April 22, 2014, http://www.supremecourt.gov/opinions/13pdf/12-682_8759.pdf.

12 Jennifer R. Holladay, "On Racism and White Privilege," from *White Anti-Racist Activism: A Personal Roadmap* (Roselle, NJ: Crandall, Dostie & Douglass Books, 2000), available online at Teaching Tolerance, http://www.tolerance.org/article/racism-and-white-privilege.

12–13 Peggy McIntosh, "White Privilege and Male Privilege (1988)," College Art Association, accessed April 8, 2016, http://www.collegeart.org/pdf/diversity/white-privilege-and-male-privilege.pdf.

13 Whitney Dow, Whiteness Project, accessed April 2016, http://whitenessproject.org/millennials/makenna-21.

13 David Edwards, "Study: White People React to Evidence of White Privilege by Claiming Personal Hardships," *AlterNet*, September 29, 2015, http://www.alternet.org/news-amp-politics/study-white-people-react-evidence-white-privilege-claiming-greater-personal.

13 Holladay, "On Racism."

14 Brittney Cooper, "In Defense of Black Rage: Michael Brown, Police and the American Dream," *Salon*, August 12, 2014, http://www.salon

.com/2014/08/12/in_defense_of
_black_rage_michael_brown
_police_and_the_american_dream/.

14 Dr24hours, Twitter post,
December 3, 2014, 5:36 p.m.,
https://twitter.com/Dr24hours.

14 Her Majesty, Twitter post,
December 3, 2014, 5:17 p.m.,
https://twitter.com/Auragasmic.

14 "Racial Profiling," ACLU.

15 Ilya Somin, "Obama
Administration Decides to
Continue the Use of Racial
Profiling in Immigration Law
Enforcement," *Washington Post*,
December 7, 2014, https://www
.washingtonpost.com/news/volokh
-conspiracy/wp/2014/12/07/obama
-administration-decides-to
-continue-racial-profiling-in
-immigration-law-enforcement/.

15 Dan Washburn, "*New York Times*
Asks, 'Is Racial or Religious
Profiling Ever Justified?,'" Asia
Society, April 15, 2011, http://
asiasociety.org/blog/asia/new-york
-times-asks-racial-or-religious
-profiling-ever-justified.

15–16 Mathias Risse and Richard
Zeckhauser, "Racial Profiling,"
Philosophy & Public Affairs 32,
no. 2 (April 2004): 131–170, http://
onlinelibrary.wiley.com/doi/10
.1111/j.1088-4963.2004.00009.x
/full.

16 Randy Wimbley, "Trooper Claims
State Police Policies Encourage
Racial Profiling," *Fox 2*, last
modified March 18, 2016, http://
www.fox2detroit.com/news/local
-news/109458270-story.

17 "Legal Scholar: Jim Crow Still
Exists in America," *NPR*, January
16, 2012, http://www.npr.org/2012
/01/16/145175694/legal-scholar-jim
-crow-still-exists-in-america.

17 "The Hunted and the Hated: An
Inside Look at the NYPD's Stop-
and-Frisk Policy," *Nation* video,
8:08–9:54, October 9, 2012, available
online at "The NYPD Officers Who
See Racial Bias in the NYPD," http://
www.theatlantic.com/national
/archive/2015/01/the-nypd-officers
-who-see-racial-bias-in-the-nypd
/384106.

18 Emily Badger, "The Long, Halting,
Unfinished Fight to End Racial
Profiling in America," *Washington
Post*, December 4, 2014, https://www
.washingtonpost.com/news/wonk/wp
/2014/12/04/the-long-halting
-unfinished-fight-to-end-racial
-profiling-in-america/.

19 Ron Nixon, "Minnesota T.S.A.
Manager Says He Was Told to Target
Somali-Americans," *New York Times*,
April 27, 2016, http://www.nytimes
.com/2016/04/28/us/politics/minnesota
-tsa-manager-says-he-was-told-to
-target-somali-americans.html.

19 "Racial Profiling," ACLU.

20 Frederick Douglass to William Lloyd
Garrison, May 23, 1846, The Gilder
Lehrman Center for the Study of
Slavery, Resistance, and Abolition,
Yale University, http://glc.yale.edu
/letter-william-lloyd-garrison-may
-23-1846.

25 "Fourteenth Amendment," US
Constitution, Cornell University Law
School, accessed June 6, 2016, https://
www.law.cornell.edu/constitution
/amendmentxiv.

26 James L. Conyers, ed., *Charles H.
Houston: An Interdisciplinary Study
of Civil Rights Leadership* (Lanham,
MD: Lexington Books, 2012), 105.

27 "Laws to Criminalize Black Life?,"
Slavery by Another Name, PBS video,
accessed June 15, 2016, http://www
.pbs.org/tpt/slavery-by-another-name
/themes/black-codes.

28 Beverly Guy-Sheftall, *Words of Fire: An Anthology of African-American Feminist Thought* (New York: New Press, 1995), 71.

29 Mark Berman, "Even More Black People Were Lynched in the U.S. Than Previously Thought, Study Finds," *Washington Post*, February 10, 2015, http://www.washingtonpost.com/news/post-nation/wp/2015/02/10/even-more-black-people-were-lynched-in-the-u-s-than-previously-thought-study-finds.

30 "Racial Profiling: Definition," ACLU.

32 "Teaching with Documents: Documents and Photographs Related to Japanese Relocation during WWII," National Archives, accessed July 28, 2015, https://www.archives.gov/education/lessons/japanese-relocation/.

32 Jacobus tenBroek, Edward N. Barnhart, and Floyd W. Matson, *Prejudice, War, and the Constitution: Causes and Consequences of the Evacuation of the Japanese Americans in World War II* (Berkeley: University of California Press, 1975), 110.

34 Jamelle Bouie, "A Tax on Blackness," *Slate*, May 13, 2015, http://www.slate.com/articles/news_and_politics/politics/2015/05/racism_in_real_estate_landlords_redlining_housing_values_and_discrimination.html.

36 "Interview with Robin Kelley: Legacies of Emmett Till," *American Experience*, accessed June 3, 2016, http://www.pbs.org/wgbh/amex/till/sfeature/sf_kelley_06.html.

36 William Bradford Huie, "The Shocking Story of Approved Killing in Mississippi," *Look*, January 1956, http://law2.umkc.edu/faculty/projects/ftrials/till/confession.html.

38 Andrew Cohen, "The Speech That Shocked Birmingham the Day after the Church Bombing," *Atlantic*, September 13, 2013, http://www.theatlantic.com/national/archive/2013/09/the-speech-that-shocked-birmingham-the-day-after-the-church-bombing/279565/.

38 "'Segregation Forever': A Fiery Pledge Forgiven, but Not Forgotten," *NPR*, January 14, 2013, http://www.npr.org/2013/01/14/169080969/segregation-forever-a-fiery-pledge-forgiven-but-not-forgotten.

40 Douglas Martin, "Mildred Loving, Who Battled Ban on Mixed-Race Marriage, Dies at 68," *New York Times*, May 6, 2008, http://www.nytimes.com/2008/05/06/us/06loving.html.

42 Jacqueline Bobo, Cynthia Hudley, and Claudine Michel, eds., *The Black Studies Reader* (New York: Routledge, 2004), 354.

43–44 Dan Baum, "Legalize It All: How to Win the War on Drugs," *Harper's Magazine*, April 2016, http://harpers.org/archive/2016/04/legalize-it-all/.

44 Jonathan Easley, "The Day the Drug War Really Started," *Salon*, June 19, 2011, http://www.mapinc.org/drugnews/v11/n404/a07.html.

45 Geneva Horse Chief, "Amnesty International Hears Testimony on Racial Profiling," *Indian Country Today Media Network*, October 16, 2003, http://indiancountrytodaymedianetwork.com/2003/10/16/amnesty-international-hears-testimony-racial-profiling-89442.

46 Seth Mydans, "The Police Verdict: Los Angeles Policemen Acquitted in Taped Beating," *New York Times*, April 30, 1992, https://www.nytimes.com/books/98/02/08/home/rodney-verdict.html.

46 Ibid.

46 Jeff Wallenfeldt, "Los Angeles Riots of 1992," *Encyclopaedia Britannica*, last modified January 5, 2015, http://www .britannica.com/event/Los-Angeles -Riots-of-1992.

47 Ibid.

49 Elizabeth Stuart, "Latino Activists Push for Anti-Racial-Profiling Law in Arizona," *Phoenix New Times*, September 10, 2015.

49 "Trump Stands by Statements on Mexican Illegal Immigrants, Surprised by Backlash," *FoxNews.com*, July 4, 2015, http://www.foxnews.com/politics /2015/07/04/trump-stands-by-views -dangerous-mexican-illegal -immigrants-admits-surprised-by.html.

51 Kirk Semple, "'I'm Frightened': After Attacks in Paris, New York Muslims Cope with a Backlash," *New York Times*, November 25, 2015, http:// www.nytimes.com/2015/11/26 /nyregion/im-frightened-after-paris -terrorist-attacks-new-york-city -muslims-cope-with-a-backlash.html.

52 Kirk Semple, "Young Muslim Americans Are Feeling the Strain of Suspicion," *New York Times*, December 14, 2015, http://www.nytimes.com /2015/12/15/nyregion/young-muslim -americans-are-feeling-the-strain-of -suspicion.html.

52 Liz Robbins, "'Do You Know Me? Do You Know My Heart?,'" *New York Times*, December 10, 2015, http://www .nytimes.com/interactive/2015/12/10 /nyregion/muslims-in-new-york-react -to-donald-trump.html.

53 John M. Glionna, "Civil Rights Lawyer Seeks to Commemorate Another Side of Southern Heritage: Lynchings," *Los Angeles Times*, July 5, 2015, http://www.latimes.com /nation/la-na-alabama-lynchings -20150705-story.html.

55 US Department of Education, "Joint 'Dear Colleague' Letter," January 8, 2014, http://www2 .ed.gov/about/offices/list/ocr /letters/colleague-201401-title-vi .html#ftn7.

55–56 Dana Liebelson, "Yes, US Schools Still Discipline Students Based on Their Race," *Week*, January 23, 2014, http://theweek.com/articles /452625/yes-schools-still-discipline -students-based-race.

58 Sarah Kaplan and Abby Phillip, "'They Thought It Was a Bomb': 9th-Grader Arrested after Bringing a Home-Built Clock to School," *Washington Post*, September 16, 2015, http://www .washingtonpost.com/news /morning-mix/wp/2015/09/16 /they-thought-it-was-a-bomb -ahmed-mohamed-texas-9th -grader-arrested-after-bringing-a -home-built-clock-to-school.

58 Manny Fernandez and Christine Hauser, "Handcuffed for Making Clock, Ahmed Mohamed, 14, Wins Time with Obama," *New York Times*, September 16, 2015, http:// www.nytimes.com/2015/09/17/us /texas-student-is-under-police -investigation-for-building-a-clock .html.

58 Ken Kalthoff, "Irving Teen Says He's Falsely Accused of Making a 'Hoax Bomb,'" *NBC DFW.com*, September 18, 2015, http://www .nbcdfw.com/news/local/Irving -Student-Says-Hes-Falsely -Accused-of-Making-a-Hoax-Bomb -327794401.html.

58 Clary Ritger, "Why Racial Integration Is Still a Problem on Today's Campus," *USA Today*, March 11, 2013, http://college .usatoday.com/2013/03/11/why-racial -integration-is-still-a-problem-on -todays-campus/.

59 Jordyn Holman, "Opinion: What Students of Color Are Fighting for on College Campuses," *Los Angeles Times*, November 17, 2015, http://www.latimes.com/opinion/opinion-la/la-ol-students-college-campus-racism-20151117-story.html.

59 Catherine Long, "What It's Like to Be Black on Campus: Isolated, Exhausted, Calling for Change," *Seattle Times*, April 9, 2016, http://www.seattletimes.com/seattle-news/education/what-its-like-to-be-black-on-campus-isolating-exhausting-calling-for-change/.

60 Kiyun Kim, "Racial Microaggressions: Selected Works," Kimkiyun.com, accessed April 4, 2016, http://kimkiyun.com/#/fine-art/microaggressions.

60 Tori DeAngelis, "Unmasking 'Racial Micro Aggressions,'" *American Psychological Association* 40, no. 2 (2009): 42, http://www.apa.org/monitor/2009/02/microaggression.aspx.

61 Tanya Figueroa and Sylvia Hurtado, "Underrepresented Racial and/or Ethnic Minority (URM) Graduate Students in STEM Disciplines: A Critical Approach to Understanding Graduate School Experiences and Obstacles to Degree Progression," Association for the Study of Higher Education, November 2013, 22, http://imsd.emory.edu/documents/documents-pdfs/ASHE2013-URM-Grad-Students-in-STEM.pdf.

61 Michael Luo, "In Job Hunt, College Degree Can't Close Racial Gap," November 30, 2009, *New York Times*, http://www.nytimes.com/2009/12/01/us/01race.html.

62 John Blake, "The New Threat: 'Racism without Racists,'" *CNN*, last modified November 27, 2014, http://www.cnn.com/2014/11/26/us/ferguson-racism-or-racial-bias/.

63 Gabriel Medina Arenas, "Mexicans in US Feel Prejudice on All Sides," *Nebraska Mosaic*, July 25, 2012, http://cojmc.unl.edu/mosaic/2012/07/25/mexicans-u-s-feel-discrimination-sides/.

64 Bao Phi, "Brutal," *A Good Time for the Truth: Race in Minnesota*, ed. Sun Yung Shin (Saint Paul: Minnesota Historical Society Press, 2016) 84.

65 Paul Kiel, "Debt and the Racial Wealth Gap," *New York Times*, December 31, 2015, http://www.nytimes.com/2016/01/03/opinion/debt-and-the-racial-wealth-gap.html.

67 Chris Gentilviso, "Ken Emanuelson, Texas Tea Party Activist, Calls GOP Black Voter Comments 'A Mistake,'" *Huffington Post*, last modified June 5, 2013, http://www.huffingtonpost.com/2013/06/04/ken-emanuelson-tea-party-_n_3386884.html.

68 DW Gibson, "'I Put in White Tenants': The Grim, Racist (and Likely Illegal) Methods of One Brooklyn Landlord," *New York Magazine*, May 12, 2015, http://nymag.com/daily/intelligencer/2015/05/grim-racist-methods-of-one-brooklyn-landlord.html.

69–70 Todd Hollingshead, "Minority Entrepreneurs Face Discrimination When Seeking Loans," *Brigham Young University News*, May 28, 2014, https://news.byu.edu/news/minority-entrepreneurs-face-discrimination-when-seeking-loans.

70 Steve Volk, "Racial Profiling on the Main Line," *Philadelphia*, November 22, 2015, http://www.phillymag.com/articles/racial-profiling-main-line/#rsRJd6IQ298tibLD.99.

71 "Lead Poisoning and Health," World Health Organization, August 2015, http://www.who.int/mediacentre/factsheets/fs379/en.

72 Ronald M. Wyatt, "Has Racism Found a Way into Our Health Care System?," KevinMD.com, August 24, 2015, http://www.kevinmd.com/blog/2015/08/has-racism-found-a-way-into-our-health-care-system.html.

73–74 Editorial board, "The Racism at the Heart of Flint's Crisis," *New York Times*, March 25, 2016, http://www.nytimes.com/2016/03/25/opinion/the-racism-at-the-heart-of-flints-crisis.html.

74 Julia Craven and Tyler Tynes, "The Racist Roots of Flint's Water Crisis," *Huffington Post*, last modified February 3, 2016, http://www.huffingtonpost.com/entry/racist-roots-of-flints-water-crisis_us_56b12953e4b04f9b57d7b118.

75 Blake, "The New Threat."

76 "Fourteenth Amendment," US Constitution.

78 "US: Drug Arrests Skewed by Race," Human Rights Watch, March 2, 2009, https://www.hrw.org/news/2009/03/02/us-drug-arrests-skewed-race.

78 Tierney Sneed, "School Resource Officers: Safety Priority or Part of the Problem?," *US News*, January 30, 2015, http://www.usnews.com/news/articles/2015/01/30/are-school-resource-officers-part-of-the-school-to-prison-pipeline-problem.

79 Ibid.

79 Eliott C. McLaughlin, "Texas Student Tased by Police Exits Coma, Enters Rehabilitation, Attorney Says," *CNN*, last modified February 3, 2014, http://www.cnn.com/2014/01/31/us/texas-taser-high-school-student-coma.

83 "Opinion and Order: David Floyd, Lalit Clarkson, Deon Dennis, and David Ourlicht, individually and on behalf of a class of all others similarly situated, Plaintiffs, against The City of New York, Defendant," 3, United States District Court, Southern District of New York, August 12, 2013, http://www.nysd.uscourts.gov/cases/show.php?db=special&id=317.

83 Ibid., 94.

83 Ibid., 3.

84 "Stop and Frisk in Chicago," ACLU of Illinois, March 2015, 1, http://www.aclu-il.org/wp-content/uploads/2015/03/ACLU_StopandFrisk_6.pdf.

85 "Police Video Shows Sandra Bland's 85," *New York Times* video, 6:15, July 22, 2015, http://www.nytimes.com/video/us/100000003813646/police-video-shows-sandra-blands-arrest.html.

85 Katie Rogers, "The Death of Sandra Bland: Questions and Answers," *New York Times*, July 23, 2015, http://www.nytimes.com/interactive/2015/07/23/us/23blandlisty.html.

86 Samer Hijazi, "Arab Americans Claim Police Brutality in Dearborn Heights," *Arab American News*, May 26, 2016, http://www.arabamericannews.com/news/news/id_12298/Arab-Americans-claim-police-brutality-in-Dearborn-Heights.html.

86–87 Sharon LaFraniere and Andrew W. Lehren, "The Disproportionate Risks of Driving While Black," *New York Times*, October 24, 2015, http://www.nytimes.com/2015/10/25/us/racial-disparity-traffic-stops-driving-black.html.

88–89 Randal C. Archibold, "Arizona Enacts Stringent Law on

Immigration," *New York Times*,
April 23, 2010, http://www.nytimes
.com/2010/04/24/us/politics
/24immig.html.

89 Brian Knowlton, "Calderón
Again Assails Arizona Law on
Detention," *New York Times*, May
20, 2010, http://www.nytimes
.com/2010/05/21/world/americas
/21calderon.html.

89 Roberto Lovato, "Arizona's
Immigrants under 'Reasonable
Suspicion,'" *Nation*, June 26, 2012,
https://www.thenation.com/article
/arizonas-immigrants-under
-reasonable-suspicion.

92 Jake Halpern, "The Cop," *New
Yorker*, August 10 and 17, 2015,
http://www.newyorker.com
/magazine/2015/08/10/the-cop.

92 Michelle Ye Hee Lee, "'Hands
Up, Don't Shoot' Did Not Happen
in Ferguson," *Washington Post*,
March 19, 2015, https://www
.washingtonpost.com/news/fact
-checker/wp/2015/03/19/hands-up
-dont-shoot-did-not-happen-in
-ferguson.

93 Halpern, "The Cop."

93 Ibid.

93 Mark Berman and Wesley Lowery,
"The 12 Key Highlights from the
DOJ's Scathing Ferguson Report,"
Washington Post, March 4, 2015,
https://www.washingtonpost.com
/news/post-nation/wp/2015/03/04
/the-12-key-highlights-from-the
-dojs-scathing-ferguson-report.

93 Bijan Stephen, "The Talk: How
Black Parents Prepare Their
Young Sons for Life in America,"
Matter, August 20, 2014, https://
medium.com/matter/the-talk
-92371a1c0ae5#.12h6criho.

95 Jorge Rivas, "Cellmate Charged with
Murder in Death of Native American
Activist," *Fusion*, August 4, 2015,
http://fusion.net/story/17731/cellmate
-charged-with-jail-death-of-native
-american-activist/.

96 Joshua Berlinger, "Police Release
Timeline of Events Leading up to
Freddie Gray's Death," *CNN*, last
modified April 23, 2015, http://www
.cnn.com/2015/04/20/us/freddie-gray
-baltimore-timeline.

97 Racial Profiling and Freddie Gray,"
Baltimore Sun, August 25, 2015,
http://www.baltimoresun.com/news
/opinion/bs-ed-frosh-profiling
-20150825-story.html.

97 Kevin Rector and Jean Marbella,
"Friends, Neighbors Say Freddie
Gray Was a Well-Liked Jokester
Known to Police," *Baltimore Sun*,
April 21, 2015, http://www
.baltimoresun.com/news/maryland
/baltimore-city/bs-md-freddie-gray
-profile-20150420-story.html.

100 Greg Botelho and Holly Yan, "George
Zimmerman Found Not Guilty of
Murder in Trayvon Martin's Death,"
CNN, July 14, 2013, http://www.cnn
.com/2013/07/13/justice/zimmerman
-trial.

102 Ta-Nehisi Coates, "In God We
Trust—but We Have Put Our Faith
in Our Guns," *Atlantic*, February 3,
2014, http://www.theatlantic.com
/politics/archive/2014/02/in-god-we
-trust-but-we-have-put-our-faith-in
-our-guns/283534.

102 Erin Meisenzahl-Peace, "Stand Your
Ground Laws Are Racist, New Study
Reveals," *Broadly*, December 1, 2015,
https://broadly.vice.com/en_us
/article/stand-your-ground-laws-are
-racist-new-study-reveals.

103 Alan Blinder and Marc Santora,
"Officer Who Killed Walter Scott Is

Fired, and Police Chief Denounces Shooting," *New York Times*, April 8, 2015, http://www.nytimes.com /2015/04/09/us/walter-scott-shooting -video-stopped-case-from-being -swept-under-rug-family-says.html.

103 Ibid.

104 "A Review of the Preliminary Report and Recommendations," American Bar Association, National Task Force on Stand Your Ground Laws, August 8, 2014, http://www.americanbar .org/content/dam/aba/administrative /racial_ethnic_justice/aba_natl_task _force_on_syg_laws_preliminary _report_program_book.authcheckdam .pdf.

105 Jeremey Johnson, "The Reason I Can't Have White Friends: Race Talk in America," *Huffington Post*, August 6, 2015, http://www.huffingtonpost .com/jeremey-johnson/the-reason-i -cant-have-wh_1_b_7928498.html.

106 "Legal Scholar," *NPR*.

107 Lisa Trei, "'Black' Features Can Sway in Favor of Death Penalty," *Stanford News*, May 3, 2006, http://news .stanford.edu/news/2006/may3 /deathworthy-050306.html.

107 Linda Myers, "When Victims Are White, Stereotypes of Blacks Influence Who Gets Death Penalty, New Study Shows," *Cornell Chronicle*, June 15, 2006, http://www .news.cornell.edu/stories/2006/06 /defendants-blackness-influences -death-sentences.

107 Trei, "'Black' Features."

108 "'I Can't Breathe,' Eric Garner Put in Chokehold by NYPD Officer— Video," *Guardian* (US ed.) video, 0:44–2:48, December 4, 2014, http:// www.theguardian.com/us-news/video /2014/dec/04/i-cant-breathe-eric -garner-chokehold-death-video.

108 S. E. Smith, "Asthma Didn't Kill Eric Garner—Racism Did," *Daily Dot*, last modified December 11, 2015, http://www .dailydot.com/opinion/eric -garner-victim-blaming/.

108 Abby Ohlheiser, Elahe Izadi, and Cameron Barr, "N.Y. Grand Jury Declines to Indict Officer in Death of Eric Garner, Igniting Protests," *Washington Post*, December 3, 2014, https:// www.washingtonpost.com /politics/2014/12/03/8dc55084 -7b2b-11e4-84d4-7c896b90abdc _story.html.

109 David A. Love, "Dealing with the Racial Nature of Wrongful Convictions," *Huffington Post*, December 23, 2014, http://www .huffingtonpost.com/david-a -love/dealing-with-the-racial -nature-of-wrongful-convictions _b_6337850.html.

110 Kari Huus, "Muslim Travelers Say They're Saddled with 9/11 Baggage," *Today*, last modified September 9, 2011, http://www .today.com/id/44334738/ns /today-today_news/t/muslim -travelers-say-theyre-still -saddled-baggage/# .VpiKTFJsQlZ.

111–112 Benjamin Weiser, "Lawsuit over New York Police Surveillance of Muslims Is Revived," *New York Times*, October 13, 2015, http:// www.nytimes.com/2015/10/14 /nyregion/appeals-court -reinstates-lawsuit-over-police -surveillance-of-muslims.html.

113 Ayesha Durrani, "Leaving the Bubble," *Huffington Post*, February 26, 2016, http://www .huffingtonpost.com/ayesha -durrani/leaving-the-bubble _b_9301908.html.

113 Michael S. Schmidt, "Racial Profiling Rife at Airport, U.S. Officers Say," *New York Times*, August 11, 2012, http://www.nytimes.com/2012/08/12/us/racial-profiling-at-boston-airport-officials-say.html?_r=0.

113 Khalid El Khatib, "When Racial Profiling at the Airport Has Nothing to Do with Your Appearance," *Identities.Mic*, May 4, 2015, http://mic.com/articles/117096/when-racial-profiling-at-the-airport-has-nothing-to-do-with-your-appearance#.vfK8HISO2.

114 Earl Lichtblau, "Inquiry Targeted 2,000 Foreign Muslims in 2004," *New York Times*, October 30, 2008, http://www.nytimes.com/2008/10/31/us/31inquire.html.

116 "Saeb Mokdad v. Loretta E. Lynch, Attorney General, et al.," United States Court of Appeals for the Sixth Circuit, October 2015, 2, http://www.clearinghouse.net/chDocs/public/NS-MI-0004-0003.pdf.

116 Ben Norton, "Victory over Racial Profiling: Federal Court Rules Americans Can Challenge No Fly List," *Salon.com*, October 26, 2015, http://www.salon.com/2015/10/26/victory_over_racial_profiling_federal_court_rules_americans_can_challenge_no_fly_list.

117 Itay Hod, "Hollywood Mogul Haim Saban Calls for 'More Scrutiny' of Muslims," *Wrap*, November 18, 2015, http://www.thewrap.com/hollywood-mogul-haim-saban-more-scrutiny-muslims-profiling-hillary-clinton.

117 Frances Kai-Haw Wang, "Muslim, Asian-American LGBTQ Advocates Call for Love, Solidarity after Orlando Shooting," *NBC News*, June 13, 2016, http://www.nbcnews.com/news/asian-america/muslim-asian-american-lgbtq-advocates-call-love-solidarity-orlando-shooting-n590951.

118–119 Kerry Burke, Mark Morales, Barbara Ross, and Ginger Adams Otis, "Barneys Accused Teen of Using Fake Debit Card for $349 Belt Because He's a 'Young Black Male': Lawsuit," *New York Daily News*, last modified October 24, 2013, http://www.nydailynews.com/new-york/barneys-accused-stealing-black-teen-article-1.1493101.

120 "Attorney General Holder Announces Federal Law Enforcement Agencies to Adopt Stricter Policies to Curb Profiling," United States Department of Justice, Office of Public Affairs, December 8, 2014, http://www.justice.gov/opa/pr/attorney-general-holder-announces-federal-law-enforcement-agencies-adopt-stricter-policies-0.

120 "Cardin, Conyers, Reintroduce Federal Ban on Racial Profiling by Law Enforcement," Ben Cardin, April 22, 2015, http://www.cardin.senate.gov/newsroom/press/release/cardin-conyers-reintroduce-federal-ban-on-racial-profiling-by-law-enforcement.

122 Colleen Curry, "California Cops Are Pissed about the State's New Racial Profiling Law," *Vice News*, October 6, 2015, https://news.vice.com/article/california-cops-are-pissed-about-the-states-new-racial-profiling-law.

122 Ibid.

122 Stuart, "Latino Activists."

123 Reddit Hudson, "Being a Cop Showed Me Just How Racist and Violent the Police Are. There's Only One Fix," *Washington Post*, December 6, 2014, https://www.washingtonpost.com

/posteverything/wp/2014/12/06
/i-was-a-st-louis-cop-my-peers
-were-racist-and-violent-and
-theres-only-one-fix/.

124   Richard Pérez-Peña, "University
of Cincinnati Officer Indicted
in Shooting Death of Samuel
Dubose," *New York Times*, July
29, 2015, http://www.nytimes
.com/2015/07/30/us/university
-of-cincinnati-officer-indicted
-in-shooting-death-of-motorist
.html.

124   "Review and Investigation of
Officer Raymond M. Tensing's
Use of Deadly Force on July 19,
2015: University of Cincinnati
Police Department: Summary
of Key Findings," University
of Cincinnati, August 21, 2015,
https://www.uc.edu/content/dam
/uc/safety-reform/documents
/Kroll%20Report%20of%20
Investigation%208.31.2015.pdf.

124–125   Alissa Skelton, "Omaha Police
Beef Up Efforts to Avoid
Racial Profiling," *Omaha.com*,
December 20, 2014, http://www
.omaha.com/news/metro/omaha
-police-beef-up-efforts-to-avoid
-racial-profiling/article
_63aae11a-8772-5b0b-acfd
-fb4270827f65.html.

125   Marc Mauer, "Addressing Racial
Disparities in Incarceration,"
99S, *Prison Journal*, August 25,
2011, http://sentencingproject
.org/wp-content/uploads/2016/01
/Addressing-Racial-Disparities
-in-Incarceration.pdf.

126   Nixon, "Minnesota TSA
Manager."

126   Beatrice Dupuy, "Minneapolis
Somali-American and Muslim
Leaders Speak Out against
Racial Profiling," *Minneapolis
Star Tribune*, May 2, 2016.

127   Ray Sanchez and Shimon Prokupecz,
"Protests after N.Y. Cop Not Indicted
in Chokehold Death; Feds Reviewing
Case," *CNN*, last modified December
4, 2014, http://www.cnn.com/2014/12
/03/justice/new-york-grand-jury
-chokehold.

127   Blinder and Santora, "Officer Who
Killed Walter Scott."

127   "'Profoundly Disappointed': Michael
Brown Family Reacts to Lack of
Indictment," *NBC News*, November
24, 2014, http://www.nbcnews.com
/storyline/michael-brown-shooting
/profoundly-disappointed-michael
-brown-family-reacts-lack-indictment
-n255436.

128   Nicole Hensley, "Marilyn Mosby
Announces Criminal Charges in
Death of Freddie Gray," *New York
Daily News*, last modified May 1,
2015, http://www.nydailynews.com
/news/crime/criminal-charges-filed
-freddie-gray-death-transcript-article
-1.2206744.

128   John Kass, "Ferguson a Lesson
Lost on Race," *Chicago Tribune*,
November 26, 2014, http://www
.chicagotribune.com/news/columnists
/kass/ct-kass-met-1126-20141126
-column.html.

128   Cooper, "In Defense of Black Rage."

129   Robert Stephens II, "In Defense of
the Ferguson Riots," *Jacobin*, August
14, 2014, https://www.jacobinmag
.com/2014/08/in-defense-of-the
-ferguson-riots/c.

130   "About the Black Lives Matter
Network," Black Lives Matter,
accessed May 19, 2016, http://
blacklivesmatter.com/about.

131   J. A. Adande, "Purpose of 'I Can't
Breath' T-shirts," *ESPN*, December
10, 2014, http://espn.go.com/nba
/story/_/id/12010612/nba-stars
-making-statement-wearing-breathe
-shirts.

131 Michelle Ye Hee Lee, "'Hands Up, Don't Shoot' Did Not Happen in Ferguson," *Washington Post*, March 19, 2015, https://www.washingtonpost.com/news/fact-checker/wp/2015/03/19/hands-up-dont-shoot-did-not-happen-in-ferguson.

132 Derk Brown, Twitter post, July 17, 2015, 8:51 a.m., https://twitter.com/DreadHead_46.

132 April, Twitter post, July 17, 2015, 5:54 a.m., https://twitter.com/ReignOfApril.

133 Charles M. Blow, "The Perfect-Victim Pitfall: Michael Brown, Now Eric Garner," *New York Times*, December 3, 2014, http://www.nytimes.com/2014/12/04/opinion/charles-blow-first-michael-brown-now-eric-garner.html.

133 Editorial board, "Voters Tell Prosecutors, Black Lives Matter," *New York Times*, March 18, 2016, http://www.nytimes.com/2016/03/18/opinion/voters-tell-prosecutors-black-lives-matter.html.

134 Chris Moody, "Democrats Lose Control of Presidential Event," *CNN*, July 29, 2015, http://www.cnn.com/2015/07/18/politics/bernie-sanders-netroots-nation-black-lives-matter.

134 Carol Anderson, "Ferguson Isn't about Black Rage against Cops. It's about White Rage against Progress," *Washington Post*, August 29, 2014, https://www.washingtonpost.com/opinions/ferguson-wasnt-black-rage-against-copsit-was-white-rage-against-progress/2014/08/29/3055e3f4-2d75-11e4-bb9b-997ae96fad33_story.html.

135 Clint Smith, "How to Raise a Black Son in America," TED, March 2015, http://www.ted.com/talks/clint_smith_how_to_raise_a_black_son_in_america.

135 Joshua Adams, "The Troll Named #AllLivesMatter," *Huffington Post*, last modified December 9, 2015, http://www.huffingtonpost.com/joshua-adams/alllivesmatter-needs-to-e_b_8683982.html.

136 "Test Yourself for Hidden Bias," Teaching Tolerance, accessed July 1, 2016, http://www.tolerance.org/activity/test-yourself-hidden-bias.

136 "Stereotypes and Performance Bias," video, 0:43–0:46, https://managingbias.fb.com/.

136–137 Ibid., 15:47–16:04.

137 Kali Holloway, "11 Things White People Can Do to be Real Anti-Racist Allies," *Salon*, April 29, 2015, http://www.salon.com/2015/04/29/11_things_white_people_can_do_to_be_real_anti_racist_allies_partner/.

137 Roxane Gay, "On Making Black Lives Matter," *Marie Claire*, July 11, 2016, http://www.marieclaire.com/culture/features/a21423/roxane-gay-philando-castile-alton-sterling.

139 Karen Ford, "Young Black Activists Are in It for the Long Haul," *People's World*, February 16, 2016, http://www.peoplesworld.org/young-black-activists-are-in-it-for-the-long-haul/.

Selected Bibliography

Alexander, Michelle. *The New Jim Crow: Mass Incarceration in the Age of Colorblindness*. New York: New Press, 2012.

Amnesty International USA. *Threat and Humiliation: Racial Profiling, Domestic Security, and Human Rights in the United States*. Accessed October 2, 2015. Available online at http://www.amnestyusa.org/pdfs /rp_report.pdf.

Blackmon, Douglas A. *Slavery by Another Name: The Re-Enslavement of Black Americans from the Civil War to World War II*. New York: Doubleday, 2008.

Coates, Ta-Nehisi. *Between the World and Me*. New York: Spiegel & Grau, 2015.

Du Bois, W. E. B. *The Souls of Black Folk*. New York: Dover, 1994. First published 1903 by A. C. McClurg & Co.

Ernst, Carl W., ed. *Islamophobia in America: The Anatomy of Intolerance*. New York: Palgrave MacMillan, 2013.

Glaser, Jack. *Suspect Race: Causes and Consequences of Racial Profiling*. New York: Oxford University Press, 2015.

Glover, Karen S. *Racial Profiling: Research, Racism, and Resistance*. Lanham, MD: Rowman & Littlefield, 2009.

Guy-Sheftall, Beverly. *Words of Fire: An Anthology of African-American Feminist Thought*. New York: New Press, 1995.

Muhammad, Khalil Gibran. *The Condemnation of Blackness: Race, Crime, and the Making of Modern Urban America*. Cambridge, MA: Harvard University Press, 2010.

Parks, Gregory S., and Matthew W. Hughey, eds. *12 Angry Men: True Stories of Being a Black Man in America Today*. New York: New Press, 2010.

United States Sentencing Commission. *Demographic Differences in Federal Sentencing Practices*, March 2010. Available online at http://www.albany .edu/scj/documents/USSC_Multivariate_Regression_Analysis_Report_001 .pdf.

US Department of Education Office for Civil Rights. *Civil Rights Data Collection: Data Snapshot: School Discipline*, March 21, 2014. Available online at http://ocrdata.ed.gov/Downloads/CRDC-School-Discipline -Snapshot.pdf.

Zack, Naomi. *White Privilege and Black Rights: The Injustice of U.S. Police Racial Profiling and Homicide*. Lanham, MD: Rowman & Littlefield, 2015.

Further Information

To learn more about the long and complex history of racial profiling in the United States and to keep up with the latest developments of this ever-evolving issue, consult these and other reputable sources.

Books

Bryfonski, Dedria, ed. *Islamophobia*. Current Controversies series. Detroit: Greenhaven, 2012. This volume explores issues related to Islamophobia, including the factors that contribute to a fear of Islam (Islamophobia) and whether suspicion of Islam is rational.

Gansworth, Eric. *If I Ever Get Out of Here*. New York: Arthur A. Levine, 2013. This young adult novel follows the struggles and triumphs of an American Indian teen boy growing up on a reservation in the 1970s. Against the backdrop of his community's poverty, Lewis deals with prejudice from his white peers and teachers, forms an unexpected friendship with the new white boy in school, and finds an anchor in his cultural heritage.

Grinapol, Corinne. *Racial Profiling and Discrimination: Your Legal Rights*. New York: Rosen, 2016. This book covers different types of discrimination, illustrated with real-life stories, and gives readers information on what they can do if they experience racial profiling.

Hanson-Harding, Alexandra. *Are You Being Racially Profiled?* New York: Enslow, 2016. This book addresses what racial profiling is, why it happens, whom it targets, and what someone who is at risk of racial profiling can do about it.

Jones, Patrick. *Teen Incarceration: From Cell Bars to Ankle Bracelets*. Minneapolis: Twenty-First Century, 2017. Learn how juvenile justice works in the United States. Meet the people working to reform the system and gain a better understanding of the tough realities of life behind bars.

Lentin, Alana. *Racism and Ethnic Discrimination*. New York: Rosen, 2011. This book explores a number of aspects of racism and discrimination in the United States, including politics, immigration, and more.

Merino, Noel, ed. *Racial Profiling*. Current Controversies series. Farmington Hills, MI: Greenhaven, 2015. This collection of articles explores various aspects of racial profiling, including whether racial profiling is a problem, the profiling of Muslims in the war on terror, the causes and consequences of racial profiling; and what to do about racial profiling.

Murray, Elizabeth A. *Overturning Wrongful Convictions: Science Serving Justice*. Minneapolis: Twenty-First Century Books, 2015. Since 1989 more than fourteen hundred Americans who experienced wrongful conviction have been exonerated. This book recounts stories of individuals who served someone else's prison time due to mistaken eyewitness identification, police misconduct, faulty forensic science, poor legal representation, courtroom mistakes, and other factors.

Osborne, Linda Barrett. *This Land Is Our Land: A History of American Immigration*. New York: Abrams, 2016. This exploration of immigration to the United States offers an analysis of how the past has influenced modern events and current views on immigration.

Pilgrim, David. *Understanding Jim Crow: Using Racist Memorabilia to Teach Tolerance and Promote Social Justice*. Oakland: PM, 2015. Presenting historic examples of racist posters, publications, and other objects, this book explores the history of Jim Crow and the way its supporters used caricature and propaganda to dehumanize African Americans and limit their rights.

Reynolds, Jason, and Brendan Kiely. *All American Boys*. New York: Atheneum, 2015. In this novel, two teens—one black and one white—grapple with the repercussions of a single violent act that leaves their school, their community and, ultimately, the country bitterly divided by racial tension.

Wittenstein, Vicki Oransky. *For the Good of Mankind? The Shameful History of Human Medical Experimentation*. Minneapolis: Twenty-First Century Books, 2014. Some of history's greatest medical advances have been interwoven with its most horrifying medical atrocities. Medical experimentation harmed and humiliated test subjects, many of whom were people of color with little legal recourse.

Woodson, Jacqueline. *Brown Girl Dreaming*. New York: Nancy Paulsen Books, 2014. Written in verse, this book describes Woodson's experience of growing up African American in the 1960s and 1970s.

Documentaries

Burns, Ken, David McMahon, and Sarah Burns. *The Central Park Five*. Arlington, VA: PBS, 2012. In 1989 five black and Latino teens were wrongfully convicted of raping a white woman in New York City's Central Park. This documentary explores how racial profiling and institutional racism shaped the way the police, the media, and the justice system handled their case.

Ferguson: A Report from Occupied Territory. Doral, FL: Fusion, 2015. Award-winning journalist Tim Pool visits Ferguson, Missouri, in the aftermath of Michael Brown's death at the hands of a police officer. Pool examines not only the immediate causes and fallout of Brown's shooting but also racial discrimination in the criminal justice system.

Huff, Ben, and Krissana Limlamai. *No Justice, No Peace: California's Battle against Police Brutality and Racist Violence*. Los Angeles: Liberation News, 2013. In July 2012, the killing of Manuel Diaz by a police officer ignited protests throughout Anaheim, California. A year later, citizens launched a fresh wave of activism to protest police brutality and racial discrimination. Their grassroots efforts to address injustice in their community are the focus of this documentary.

Nelson, Stanley, Jr. *The Black Panthers: Vanguard of the Revolution*. Arlington, VA: PBS, 2015. In the 1960s, young urban black Americans sought to create explosive change that would overturn racial inequality in the United States. The Black Panther Party faced off against US law enforcement and government agencies in a decades-long struggle that both challenged and fueled racial biases across the nation.

Slavery by Another Name. Arlington, VA: PBS, 2012. After slavery in the United States officially ended in 1865, other forms of legalized servitude took its place. This documentary explores how the US criminal justice system and US industries forced thousands of African Americans into a brutal system of forced labor that left a profound effect on American society.

Websites

ACLU

https://www.aclu.org

The home page of the American Civil Liberties Union offers information on racial profiling as well as many other civil rights issues.

Mapping Police Violence

http://mappingpoliceviolence.org

This website tracks the number of black Americans killed by police officers, records details of the incidents that led to these deaths, and offers analysis of the data.

NAACP

http://www.naacp.org

The website of the National Association for the Advancement of Colored People (NAACP) provides a wide range of information on race and race-related issues in the United States.

Project Implicit

https://implicit.harvard.edu/implicit

Test yourself on a wide variety of hidden biases at this website and project created by psychologists from the University of Virginia, the University of Washington, and Harvard University.

Teaching Tolerance

http://www.tolerance.org

This website from the Southern Poverty Law Center presents a wealth of information on diversity in the United States.

Understanding Prejudice: Exercises and Demonstrations

http://www.understandingprejudice.org/demos

This site provides a variety of Hidden Bias Tests and other tools to consider underlying prejudices that can affect people and their actions.

Index

About the Author

Alison Marie Behnke is a writer and editor. She has written about a wide range of topics, including immigration, world and cultural geography, ethnic cuisines, American and European history, biographies, and fashion. Her 2015 book *Up for Sale: Human Trafficking and Modern Slavery* was a Best Children's Book of the Year for the Children's Book Committee at Bank Street College, as well as an NCSS/CBC Notable Social Studies Trade Book for Young People. Behnke lives in Minneapolis.

Photo Acknowledgments